Forbidden Dimensions

PRIMITIVISM, PREHISTORY AND THE
POSTHUMAN ERA

C. G. Browne

Ravine Press
Pembrokeshire, WALES

Ravine Press
www.ravinepress.com

Book Layout ©2013 BookDesignTemplates.com

First published by Ravine Press 2013
ISBN 978-1-909882-13-3 Kindle edition

This edition published by Ravine Press 2015
ISBN 978-1-909882-18-8

Contents

Prologue... 1

Introduction 2

An Invisible Reality 6

The Truth About Ritual.. 31

Life in the Penal Colony... 55

The Growth Gutter 77

Sacred Dimensions 97

A Quantum Prehistory... 117

Death Materialized 141

Dimensional Thresholds... 168

Random Ancient Memories 199

Monumental Collapse 228

The Paradoxical Machine.. 259

Afterword... 284

Epilogue... 287

Bibliography... 288

For David

Ruth Jones

x

What has never been seen before is the erection of an entire civilization on something purely negative, on what in fact might be called an absence of principle; and it is this that gives to the modern world its abnormal character and makes of it a sort of monstrosity, only to be understood if one thinks of it as corresponding to the end of a cyclic period.

— RENÉ GUÉNON, THE CRISIS OF THE MODERN WORLD

Prologue

E ven high up on a remote Welsh mountain, we cannot escape the constant noise that civilized living creates: the faint hum of a generator, the drone of distant traffic, and aeroplanes overhead. Instead, we have to imagine the silent world that belonged to prehistoric Stone Age people. It is a world where you and your clan could walk for a hundred miles and not meet any engines or even another human being. Except you would not have known what a hundred miles was. Transport yourself back in time, say half a million years, and you will find no concept of distance relating to measurement and no concept of place relating to geography. Relationship and experience replace them. Lengths of time, quantity, and mass are absent. Progress, evolution, and complexity are non-existent. Imagine not knowing how long you have existed. You are ageless, like the mountain you stand upon, but only in terms of duration, not maturity. You look down at your hand axe and know it is the same axe you have always had. It has never changed. You have never altered it because you never needed to. Perhaps it is the same axe that you have had for a million years.

Introduction

illions of light years away—or so it seems—from the primitive Stone Age, exists the modern world of three dimensions, where we travel up and down, side to side, and back and forth. Time adds a fourth dimension that takes us along a distinct and infinite road. The past stretches out behind us into darkness. The present is here and now, albeit still travelling. The future stretches away in front of us towards an invisible horizon. Civilization alone provides the conditions for this perceived reality. Without the principles with which we have designed and built modern civilization, we would still exist in a timeless, and we might say 'otherworldly', dimension of life.

Scientific thought, materialism, and linearity preoccupy our civilized minds. These three culprits of modern thinking and perception have together resulted in the loss of primitiveness: the original principles and laws relating to human life. As a species, we once knew these laws well. Yet, here we are, racing through the twenty-first century, confident that our modern three-dimensional version of reality is the 'true' reality. And as we travel forward in time, it becomes ever more taxing for our minds to consider versions of reality that might exist beyond how we have come to believe time and space should look and feel.

The problem is, a mind can only perceive three-dimensional space if it is no longer integral to its environment. In other words, only a mind that is conscious is able to look objectively at its environment and start measuring it. Over time, we have become bystanders, observers and analyzers of our existence. We are annotators with clipboards, measuring tapes, and note-pads. But *what* do we think we are measuring? And why? What exactly are we making notes of—an unfolding universe of which we are an intrinsic part or perhaps a carefully crafted picture or stage set? This book attempts to illustrate how *true reality*, or, the state of things as they exist on Earth, is hidden within the primitive template. It is at the heart of an original and un-developed world. In this book, we will be exploring that world and it is likely that we will find it is not quite as we thought it to be.

After centuries of impressive and irrefutable arguments it appears that the proponents of Time, evolution, and three dimensions were only providing a fragment of the picture. At the beginning of the twenty-first century, we are glimpsing a future heading our way that none of the great scientific minds of recent times could have predicted. The pinnacle of human evolution is about to be realized, but it does not involve world peace, environmental sustainability or strategies for global equality and justice. It does not even commit to the preservation of our species. The climax of millions of years of advancing human intelligence involves a reinvention of the bedrock of mankind's

existence: from biological to digital. At this very moment, scientists are busy pioneering this new world; this is not fiction.
A whole new phase of life experience will arrive within the next
few decades as the extravaganza of computational development, not yet a century old, spawns an unscheduled paradigm
shift. We will have reached the end of linear time in the form
of a *technological singularity*.

As well as the peace and quiet, the formidable life skills that
belonged to our Palaeolithic ancestors have also taken quite a
battering from rational three-dimensional living over the last
few millennia. Perhaps now is a good time to start reacquaint-
ing ourselves with some of those qualities, considering rational
three-dimensional living is looking rather frayed around the
edges, and in some quarters of the globe quite wretched indeed.
As the posthuman era looms, the idea of ridding our lives of
such wretchedness will no doubt seduce us. A non-physical,
disease-free, hunger-free (but not discrimination- or war-free)
world is bound to sound utopianly attractive. But we know
from past experience that terrible suffering such as we see in
the world today makes us vulnerable to accepting rather un-
sound solutions to that suffering. Many great revolutions in human social life, such as the Neolithic Revolution, have been sold
to us in retrospect on similar grounds. This book will attempt
to illustrate this point. The truth is, as the door to this invisible
and alien existence starts to open, we are utterly unprepared for
what we will find on the other side. We do not consider that
life in this virtual future might be more reminiscent of a timeless and mythical era from the deeper past, than the one of

physical three dimensions that we have spent centuries asserting is the one and only true reality. Timelessness, ritualized behaviour, and reciprocal exchange are part of the fabric of primitive life. This is a life we knew for millions of years, but it has not come to an end. It continues to exist in another dimension, a *forbidden dimension,* which at this moment in time seems ages away in our prehistoric past. This book travels some of those ages in search of the lost world of our ancient ancestors, our true selves, and nature's primitive laws, which are at the heart of all life on Earth, and perhaps beyond.

CHAPTER 1

An Invisible Reality

'The immaterial has become immaterial'
Lord Becket, Disney's Pirates of the Caribbean

I magine that Palaeolithic man is not extinct but continues to exist in a world we cannot see. We will call this invisible world the 'primitive dimension', the *original* and *underived* version of reality within which all life on Earth once occurred. Within this lifeworld, we would experience only the basic primitive laws of nature. There would be no time or space as we perceive it today, and no abstract illusions or concepts relating to what we believe is 'real'. We would find only the fundamental principles of life and society relating to tribal community and the transformational process of birth, growth, and death. Everything within this simple realm is interrelated and abides by strict laws so that it remains intact. This primitive code is bound by what we will call the *integrity principle*. This is an instinctive, unconscious behaviour that keeps people integrated with everything in their lives—the family, the clan, and the natural world around them.

The anti-evolution revolution

On the other hand, in the dimension or version of reality that modern humans frequent, our million-year-old man might be called *Homo ergaster* (work man). He exists only in the past as part of a linear sequence of events—human evolution—which exists in time and stretches on into infinity.

Homo ergaster is a primitive human species who existed in the same form for over a million years. His physical appearance, tools, and behaviour hardly changed. He lived and died in the same way for an astonishing one million years until he finally disappeared about half a million years ago. His inability to evolve over such a long period is an extraordinary fact that is largely unremarked upon in textbooks. Our culture does not regard *not* changing as phenomenal or worthy of comment. In fact, most archaeologists find the 'monotony' and 'variable sameness' of *Homo ergaster* very boring indeed. But in this story we will reflect—considering the frantic pace of change we have reached today—on what it means to stay the same for so long. We will also wonder at how primitive tribespeople who exist in the world now continue to demonstrate a similar mindset.

Thousands of years ago, primitive humans barely changed. In fact, they made it their business not to. Just as trees do not change, oceans do not change, and mountains do not change, wild prehistoric humans did not veer away from their original function. Worldwide, tribal communities exhibit the same tendency as they struggle to hold on to their traditions in the face of modern progress and development. Many are unable to acclimatize to civilized culture, even if they have accepted their integration within it. The primitive qualities these people share mean they are no different from their ancestors. In fact, to be just as their ancestors were is the crux of their existence. They do not attempt to digress from the integrity of their environment. Time as we experience it does not exist for them, just as it didn't in the Stone Age. Civilized humans created linear time to *serve* progress and development, the very things that primitive people are instinctively driven to avoid.

Homo ergaster will be our ambassador for non-change in this story. He hails from the million-year-long Acheulean hand-axe tradition. This is a period starting from about 1.8 million years ago and identified mainly by the teardrop-shaped, stone hand axe that stretched three continents of the globe and that we typically associate with Stone Age man. *Homo ergaster* was, in evolutionary terms, a 'true human'. He looked like us. He was not hairy or ape-like. He had a large, chinless face, and the heavy brow we often associate with primitive man was slight. He was tall and dark, of slender build, and lived in small nomadic bands across Africa and Asia. He died out just over half a million years ago.

Homo ergaster thrived for such a prodigious age by adhering to primitive laws that exist within the natural world. We will be exploring many of these in the chapters to come. Primitive people can only maintain these laws or principles within the social make-up of a hunting and gathering tribe or clan. Primitive communities are primarily different from those of civilized construction because they are organized in a way that they *cannot* change. In primitive life, the inability to develop is not a design flaw but a constitutional necessity. From this simple perspective, it then becomes dubious whether the intense social complexity we live with today has evolved from the simplicity and egalitarianism of this ancient human. These two lifestyles—tribal and civilized—consist of obviously conflicting principles. The different centres around which they orbit do not relate to each other, so it is difficult to see how one has developed out of the other. The viewpoint I am presenting here, and one that we will investigate, is that primitive tribal principles exist as the original template for a lifeworld in which it is *impossible* to change. The concept of development is not part of the structure of that reality, in a psychological or a physical sense. Hence, the capacity for *not changing* cannot have *evolved* to accommodate the opposite: a process of exponential development that is the basis for life in the modern world. Therefore, we are left to conclude that modernity must have been constructed from something other than, or in addition to, primitive life. This is an idea we will continue to explore throughout the book.

In general, a primitive version of life stays intact by ensuring its inhabitants avoid anything that threatens its integrity or completeness. We could see it like a vacuum, a space devoid of matter. In that space are experiences, relationships, patterns of thought, intentionality, and instinct, which combine to create an interdependent and self-sufficient world. If anything or anyone violates the principles that are within its construction, this vacuum will rupture. In a civilized environment, such an intuitive and 'of the senses' quality of life is unable to thrive. This is in part because we focus solely on the physical components of our world. As well, civilized humans have become especially uncooperative as a species. We have eliminated our ability to function within an intuitive collective, yet it is a function that most other species on this primitive Earth continue to perform.

Linear time also causes modern minds a few problems when we are trying to understand the origins of human life. Living with the arrow of time, as we do, forces us to look at this primitive dimension in terms of millions of years ago. But we could ask ourselves, did *Homo ergaster* live a million years ago or *does* he live a million years ago? What does 'a million years' mean in an age when humans have not yet invented measurements of time? The primitive existence we are searching for is timeless, full of imagery and relationships that are bursting with meaning. It is a place where voids filled with weeks, minutes, and hours are unimaginable. Our million-year-old man still exists in this realm. He stands proud and unchanged upon the mountain, listening to messages travelling on the wind. They are telling him that somewhere, just a breath away, there is a world imprisoned in a single moment of time.

Access denied!

We are looking for a dimension that is original and which does not entertain linear time. But because we live in a dimension that is composed of time, we have to travel back through time to the past to find it. Yet such a journey is not easy to undertake. In fact, we are likely to find it is quite impossible. As well as issues of time and linearity, there are also other psychological difficulties we will have to address. Our minds, having developed the levels of complexity that they have, are incapable of travelling back in time to an era of such profound simplicity. Instead, we drag our primitive ancestors through the millennia to where we are now and start to apply clumsy ideas and concepts that do not fit their psychological profile.

The philosophical theory of dualism is one such concept. The idea that matter and spirit, body and mind, are separate states that cannot blend has existed for thousands of years. It is a concept ingrained in Western culture and mandatory for the existence of the materialistic and religious global society that we have built. Yet dualism is a philosophical idea and not a fact of natural life, which most atheists and materialists will be quick to point out. One of the handicaps caused by dualism from a primitive point of view is that any vitality other than what science explains on one hand and what religion explains on the other is no longer fashionable to consider.

However, *Homo ergaster* was unconscious and integral to his environment, so his interest was *not* solely in his functional and biological well-being. But nor was it in a two-world split of spirit and matter. The only way we can be unconscious and integral to everything around us is by *relating* to everything around us using our instincts. Ancient primitive people's perception of the world would have involved animism. Animism is the belief that all things animate and inanimate have an intention of their own. There is no boundary between the physical world and the spiritual or 'other' world. Animism is difficult for modern minds to comprehend. It is the language of the ancients, of myths, of hunter-gatherer nomads—our million-year-old man would have seen intention in most things. This method of communicating with the world is still at work in many remote tribes around the globe today, who limit their contact with modern life. It is worth noting that, for a primitive mind, perceiving intention in an inanimate object does not involve projecting ourselves onto it or *anthropomorphizing*. Animism is an instinctive language that primitive people use to interact with their environment and their ancestors. To these people, it is a language inextricable from their existence.

> 'Myths are not only components of life; they are part of every individual person. To take away a man's tale is tantamount to taking away his life. Such myths have inherent economic and social functions, and this is not a local phenomenon, this is a law...Without its myths a tribe would not be able to perpetuate itself.' *Vladimir Propp, Theory and History of Folklore*

The difficulty we have as observers of this way of life is that any evidence of animism is always second hand because we are unable to experience it for ourselves. Civilized minds view animism, at best as a quaint belief system of native peoples, at worst as the childish musings of an inferior race. It is, however, an indicator of profound primitiveness within indigenous peoples. It is only found today in a few isolated pockets of the world. Their 'world of spirits' is not a primitive or pagan religion, nor is it simply a belief system. It is a natural perception of the world that exists when people remain innately integral to their environment.

> 'What the anthropologist calls a cosmology is, for the people themselves, a lifeworld.' *Tim Ingold, The Perception of the Environment*

Therefore, it is not the case that this animistic state of mind is not a legitimate perception of reality. We know that as civilized people with complex, conscious minds, we can only be integral to the make-up of our observation in a most basic physical sense. After all, that is all our cultural conditioning will allow. Our conscious state of mind creates a perspective so objective that it blinds us to the very thing we are trying to understand. We cannot appreciate the primitive dimension of perception because we cannot take part in it, and if we could we would immediately lose any desire to observe it. In the end, the physical aspects of life are all we are able to share with these people. Animism is a mindset, and access is denied.

Tim Ingold describes this point thus:

> '...a double disengagement of the observer from the world. The first sets up a division between humanity and nature; the second establishes a division, within humanity, between "native" or "indigenous" people, who live in cultures, and enlightened Westerners who do not.'

If we bring animism and the *integrity principle* into this picture, it appears unjustified to see primitive people as 'disengaged' from nature just because their belief systems are not uniform. Although primitive cultures do not always share the same details within their facts of life, the *integrity principle* still applies if animism is present. Diverse primitive cultures with an animistic world view share this integrity, regardless of the details. This then places them within nature, not without. That leaves those with civilized minds alone in their separation from nature. We are able to observe and take notes, but we cannot take part. From this perspective, physical science becomes an inevitable consequence of our exclusion rather than evidence of a superior intelligence. Science is merely the perspective of a spectator.

Therefore, to try and understand a primitive ancient mind, we must accept a few alterations to the modern ideas of what is real. Animism, intention, and the presence of spirit persons are all factors alien to our culture that we must take up and get to know.

Wanted—dead or alive

If animism means that all things are in some way alive, then we can say that dualism has contributed to a perception where they all appear to be dead. The table, the walls, my pen, the cup, the lamp, to be surrounded by silent, motionless 'things' is a modern civilized experience of the world. As the generations have passed, we have even lost the ability to see the spirit in things that are obviously alive, such as trees and flowers. We would have acknowledged personality and intention in these things as recently as just a few hundred years ago.

Isaac Newton, amongst other scientists and mathematicians, sealed our fate in this regard during the seventeenth century. He pioneered a revolution in mathematical explanations regarding how the physical world works, thereby rendering our surroundings completely inert. The result of this inertia is that we now look upon nature's apparatus with no ability to communicate with it, relate to it, and with no idea how to behave within it. Primitive people might look at the wildfires that are devastating parts of southern Australia at the moment and see the spirit of fire in a rage. But why is 'he' in a rage and what should we do to appease 'him'? And what about the devastating floods we are witnessing in Europe? As the spirit of water engulfs our towns, while homes and belongings, even loved ones, are swept ruthlessly away, what is 'she' saying to us? As an animist, what do these scenarios mean? Sadly, we have no memory of ever speaking this language. As humans have developed, we have lost the ability to engage with and relate to these natural elements. They have merely become wild, random events in a world of mechanistic orderliness.

Anthropologist Nurit Bird-David's work with the southern Indian tribes, the Nayaka, has tackled some of the misconceptions associated with primitive animism that were born largely during the Victorian era. Her studies, (along with the work of others such as Ingold, Hallowell, and Woodburn), provide rare insights into authentic primitive perception. She refers to the spirits as 'superpersons' and highlights the point that an animistic world view consists of 'sharing relationships' and an interconnectedness with each other and the superpersons, or as the Nayaka call them *devaru*, with whom they share the world. These people see a hill-devaru or a stone-devaru as members of their family. They use kinship terms, such as grandmother and grandfather in relation to them, and they talk to them in a way we might talk to each other. Bird-David in her essay *Personhood, Environment and Relational Epistemology*, says:

> 'To "talk with a tree"—rather than "cut it down"—is to perceive what *it* does as one acts towards it, being aware concurrently of changes in oneself and the tree. It is expecting response and responding, growing into mutual responsiveness and, furthermore, possibly into mutual responsibility.'

To have a reciprocal relationship with our environment is the primitive way of living. How and when we chose to move away from animism and eliminate this element of exchange from our relationship with nature is a key theme of this book. I also anticipate it will affect our future as we move towards the digitization of life. By losing a primitive relationship with our surroundings, we lose the capacity to be integral to the world around us and to speak an original language. It is a language we may well find we need in the years to come. Bird-David concludes:

> '...the most intriguing question is why and how the modernist project estranged itself from the tendency to animate things, if it is indeed universal? How and why did it stigmatize "animistic language" as a child's practice, against massive evidence...to the contrary? How did it succeed in delegitimizing animism as a valid means to knowledge, constantly fending off the impulse to deploy it and regarding it as an "incurable disease"...?'

A pod of sixteen pilot whales was beached recently on the coast of Scotland. Coastguards and marine experts worked tirelessly to get them back in the water within the fatal twelve-hour time frame, but sadly all the whales died. No one knows why this family, including three calves, came to this beach to die, but because we do not speak their language we are never going to know. Instead, we assume that they have made a 'navigational error', even though we cannot detect any indication that this is the case. Primitive people are likely to interpret the intention of these creatures as a powerful omen. Perhaps they are forecasting trouble at sea, or problems relating to death, or both. They might see the omen as a message, a warning or even a protest: that the sea is no longer fit for life. To a modern mind, this may sound far-fetched, but perhaps it is no more far-

fetched than suggesting that animals as intelligent and as profi-
cient in the water as these whales have made a navigational error.

Whatever we choose to believe about why these natural
events occur or what we think they mean, to primitive people
this is the world of omens. Omens are part of a rich animistic
language. This language consists of imagery, symbolism, and
patterns that pierce the physical world from an unseen otherworld. They provide messages and guidance to many indigenous people. A vitality drives these omens, one that is abundant
in a primitive world. In the modern world of inertia, we cannot
detect this vitality. The concept of science is not set up to accommodate the *symbolic interpretation* of natural phenomena
because this perspective does not serve our current position as
a species. Our radars have, therefore, stopped searching for
signs of life at that frequency. Mathematics is now the acceptable language for making sense of the world that surrounds us.
Consequently, the nature of deconstruction that mathematical
processes impose upon the natural world prevents us from *relating* to it.

How then in an animistic dimension do so-called 'dead' objects such as my cup and my pen communicate? Can we also
include man-made objects in the world of omens? From observing primitive people who are alive today, we can conclude
that even my pen is *available* to take part in nature's network of
exchange, but it does not mean that it will. In the modern
world, so many objects and unnatural distractions surround us
that the messages are no longer able to get through. And even
if they could, we have lost the ability to translate what they are

saying. This is in part due to the impact of science. But it is also because the demands from our environment that require a response from our rational selves are deadening our primitive senses. This does not mean that the conversation is not going on, only that we are excluded from it.

Charles Darwin—another great pioneer of modern science—also contributed to the creation of a world that we experience only in a physical sense. He did not consider a metaphysical integrity between the thousands of creatures he collected and catalogued. Even during the Victorian Age, many people would still have honoured folkloric superstition. Spirits, and particularly nature's spirits such as in woodlands and waterways, mountains and caves, had not only intention but an ability to affect our lives, positively or negatively. TV documentaries that track African lions across the Sahara in search of nitrogen or primitive tribes through the Amazon jungle in search of carbohydrates are subtle examples of Darwin's legacy.

But as an Anglican Christian, Darwin did not find this transition easy. Within his work and throughout his life we see dualism extinguishing, as his Christian God and his revolutionary science became unable to coexist. As science popularized, God was suffering, but He was not the only one. Every immaterial strand of human experience, whether spiritual, psychological, artistic or philosophical, was also losing value. Over the last few centuries, mankind has observed a matter invasion. As time has passed, we have become more and more enchanted by the physical qualities of what the world has to offer, and now it is to the exclusion of all else.

However, God and science continue to battle it out in some quarters, especially in the matter of Earth's creation and the origins of being. Yet from a primitive perspective these opposing doctrines are but one and the same. Religion and science together have dissolved all traces of a primitive tenure regarding the human encounter with life. On one hand, scientists have harnessed the qualities that exist in nature, they have 'thingified' them via the process of mathematics (Stewart 1995). According to science, the formation of a drop of dew is merely a complex differential equation. On the other hand, most religions claim that their God has created the otherworldly elements which belong to the very same drop of dew, such as its beauty and sublimity. So, science and religion may disagree about how life on Earth got here in the first place, but they share their denial of a vitality within nature as a valid source of that life. Yet all human beings perceive this vitality prior to civilizing, including our ancient man. It is the foundation of an animistic mindset.

The ug factor

As we strive to understand our prehistoric ancestors, the mechanistic modern world shuts us out from realms of perception that ancient people knew well. Their light-hearted, animistic view of the world is a view we find impossible to imagine with any seriousness. It seems we have no recollection of how life looked and felt before it became the intensely spatial and material experience we have all become so used to. Yet this perception of ours is new. It has only developed over the last few hundred years, but it has impacted significantly on our ability to contemplate any other perspective of life. It has shut down

routes to other worlds. The modern physical world has replaced the primitive otherworld or at least rendered it invisible.

This leads to another issue that we need to consider regarding the perception of primitive life, and that is our preoccupa-
tion with survival, or what I have termed the 'ug factor'.
Archaeologists and anthropologists paint a picture of Palaeolithic people struggling to survive in a harsh wilderness. They
explain how they spent their time and energy hunting, tool
making, cooking, eating, mating, fighting off wild animals and
other savage tribes, and of course coping with climate change.
But if we think about it, this is what life is like for *us.* It is therefore going to be *our* experience if we were thrown into the wilderness, naked and empty-handed, and expected to survive. No
doubt we would find it an immense challenge and just getting
enough to eat would be a struggle, if not impossible. But to gain
a realistic idea of what life was like for our ancient caveman, we
need to broaden our perspective. These people had maintained
a simple, hunting and gathering lifestyle for *millions* of years.
This tells us that, far from struggling to survive, they were experts at living a wild, nomadic life. They had generations of
knowledge passed down to them from their ancestors. As humans evolve, we tend to believe that we are refining the art of
living, improving our means of existence, and conquering the
struggle with life with each generation that passes. Yet the idea
that evolution equals progress is a notion invented by Victorian
scientists. In truth, 'to evolve' is 'to develop gradually, to expand
and unfold', and not to necessarily 'improve'. Therefore, *not*
changing suggests that we are equipped with sufficient compe-
tence for a life on Earth and that we are busy living it with ease.

This idea that prehistoric people were not struggling to survive makes sense. It also leads us to wonder about their perception of the physical environment in the first place. If physical life was *not* a struggle, then their experience of and interaction with shape and form must have been different too. If we accept that they were not preoccupied simply with function and utility, and that animism was busy connecting 'things' together, how then did ancient people perceive their world in a physical sense? Did they even have physicality in the same way we do today? These are incredibly difficult questions to answer, and we must look for clues from primitive tribes who are alive today. When we study extant tribespeople, in contrast to the cumbersome physical survival we presume of ancient people, their physicality is noticeably light. Their perception of the world is dreamlike, otherworldly, compared to ours. It consists of qualities and principles and not just physical attributes. We can assume, then, that it was the same for our ancient man. We can imagine that his environment also comprised images, symbols, and patterns that would communicate with him using the language of animism. Only when we no longer speak this instinctive language does wild living become surviving. Primitive people are seamlessly attached to their environment, which in turn provides them with what they need. They organize their lives well, and they are very sociable. Individuals in the tribe work together, and that work is minimal with plenty of leisure time:

> '...hunters and gatherers work less than we do; and, rather than a continuous travail, the food quest is intermittent, leisure abundant, and there is a greater amount of sleep in the

daytime per capita per year than in any other condition of society.' *Marshall Sahlins, Stone Age Economics*

This level of connectedness provides social and psychological nourishment to primitive people. Modern people often view their lives as routine-like, harsh, and perhaps a bit boring. But if we look more closely, we find they are attached to an invisible life support. Their primitive simplicity is in effect what sustains them. For example, they approach hunting in a lighthearted way, and it involves very little stress. The animals and the hunters communicate with each other using their instincts. The wind might also speak to them. Those in the hunting party work as a team and they share the experience, perhaps like a communal dream. The point is, primitive experience is 'of the senses'. It is driven by instinct and shared intentions, with the physical side of things merely providing the imagery. Tribes today demonstrate that this is an immensely fulfilling way to experience life, so boredom is not a factor. Boredom is a civilized invention. It is a psychological response to the introduction of linearity and the creation of the 'bits in between' the main events of our lives.

Two plus two equals zero

There are psychological boundaries that primitive minds cannot cross. We can outline these boundaries, but we do not always understand them from our rational perspective. From the civilized side of the fence, we perceive these frontiers as restrictions to progress. They are cultural weaknesses that prevent people from adopting and learning new concepts and behaviour. Generic examples include literacy, numeracy, art for art's sake, and the ability to conceive of food storage (hoarding). Sometimes there are also culture-specific elements that are unable to develop. For instance, a tribe may have a method of hunting or fishing which is traditional but not especially efficient.

The primitive inability to develop is not news, but the reasons why are undetermined. Why was our ancient man unable to develop and change? Why can't profoundly primitive extant tribes learn to count or save some of today's successful hunt for tomorrow when their hunting party may not be so lucky? The Amazonian Pirahãs were taught basic numeracy every day for eight months and at the end of it none of them could conceive of the idea that one plus one equals two. Why can't primitive people learn to farm or own property without their social and spiritual fabric coming apart? To us, these scenarios combine to create a basic platform from which we live our lives. Yet there are tribes alive today (albeit extremely few) who do not have the psychological or neurological make-up to entertain anything progressive. Earlier on in this chapter, we questioned the conventional idea that modern man evolved from primitive man. If we stay with convention, then we would assume that with a persistent and determined teacher, it would only be a matter of time before a primitive mind learns to understand what it means to count to ten. But this attitude once again transports us back to the Victorian era when primitive people were seen as immature, uneducated, and inferior versions of ourselves. From a more up-to-date vantage point, we find that the primitive environment does not consist of 'things' that need 'counting', so the ability to undertake such an abstract task is absent from a primitive psychology. In order to understand the forbidden dimension we are investigating, we need to remember that mathematics is a method that civilized individuals have used to conceptualize nature. Professor Ian Stewart explains it eloquently:

> 'A number is a process that has long ago been thingified so thoroughly that everybody thinks of it as a thing.' *Nature's Numbers*

Having said that, the primitive world still contains the processes, relationships, interactions, and patterns that the mathematics describes. While we see them as abstract and therefore 'of the mind', they are also innate to the natural world that primitive people are integral to. According to mathematician Roger Penrose, 'These properties are just there.'

In the modern world, it is normal to think of numbers as concrete objects, so we do not consider that for primitive people they are superfluous. They also interfere with principles that are central to their lives. Measurement, distance, and geography are *ideas* that are incompatible with primitive life because the balance is too weighted in favour of the physical elements. The intrinsic qualities that comprise the primitive world weaken when we pay these elements too much attention. For example, your clan's camp is about a hundred metres away from an old oak tree. The relationship you have with the tree may be significant. Perhaps you and your people value its qualities—strength, reliability, and growth. Or it may have a name: the awkward tree or the lucky tree. Perhaps it is where the clan holds its meetings. Whatever the connection is, if you then measured the distance between yourself and the tree that connection would immediately weaken as your focus shifts from the values you share to the hundred metres that separate you, which are meaningless.

So we can say that mathematical principles exist in a primitive dimension but the people who live in that dimension, such as our ancient man, cannot entertain them. Any awareness of the physical details would diminish the values and relationships that keep their world intact, which brings us back to the vacuum analogy. Once the desire to manipulate nature comes into play is when mathematics becomes interesting and actually quite useful. Not only does it describe the material world but it enables us to experiment with it. It is then that the figurative vacuum is ruptured. The modern world develops through the medium of mathematics. We can redesign and reconstruct nature according to our needs and desires. But there is a price to pay. The ability to create abstract objects from natural, everyday processes destroys the mind's capacity to communicate with its surroundings. We choose not to relate to our environment but to manipulate it. We cannot have both. So, mankind's universe has become a construction site, a work in progress. But are we able to overhaul the natural world in this way *because* we have discovered mathematics? Or is it that our perception of the world has changed and the discovery of mathematics is merely an inevitable consequence of that change? From a primitive point of view, the *intention* to manipulate nature must have come first.

The hoarder next door

A lack of numeracy is one of the boundaries where we can identify the complex modern world ending and the primitive world beginning. Another of those boundaries is food storage.

The primitive law regarding food storage is another situation where the emphasis on the physical world is restricted. This law runs in close association with a non-linear perception of time. As we know, linear time is a perception of the world that accompanies the three physical dimensions. It enables us to travel through experiences in a long line of events, from birth through to death. It is rather like looking at items of clothes drying on a washing line stretching across the garden. A primitive mind experiences time very differently if it experiences it at all. It will travel cyclically as it does in nature, which we see in the seasons and the tides. But whether in a circle or a straight line, such a mind will perceive the actual travelling differently too.

If we imagine the primitive dimension as a spherical environment, with our awareness travelling the perimeter and the place of action at the centre, our perception of experience will no longer travel in a line. We would go in and out of relevant moments, rather like we do in a dream. We would not experience the 'bits in between' (or, as I also like to call them, the 'deleted scenes'), such as waiting or travelling or killing time. The ability to store food is an example of a concept that works against a centred perception of experience such as this. Storing food is a means with which we can prepare for the future. We start to worry about what will happen tomorrow. If we start to worry too intensely about what will happen tomorrow, we are no longer living in the here and now, but somewhere in the future. A centred understanding of time is such that tomorrow does not exist because it is outside the place of action at the centre. So, if we are storing food to eat tomorrow, we must be living in a place that does not exist—a *non*-place. This is likely to be how our million-year-old man would have seen the act of hoarding food, although he would not have had the complicated thought process I have just demonstrated to explain his psychology. In the same vein, his thoughts would not work in a sequence either. He is likely to have just one thought: eat. This directness comes from his undeviating connection with primitive nature and his ability to use his intuition and instinct. He has no desire or capacity to question the natural laws because for him they are innate. He does not need to know how or why something has occurred. The fact that it is occurring is all that concerns him. Anxiety—a state of mind that has devastating consequences for those living in the modern world—is linked to this sense of linearity. It is the result of being able to plan for, and so worry about, the future. In primitive communities, anxiety as a state of mind is largely non-existent.

It is when we start to question and change these laws that arguments and debates come into play about how and why everything happens. It is then that we start to feel we should be able to make decisions as individuals regarding the way we conduct ourselves. Why shouldn't we store food? In fact, now I have mentioned it, it seems ridiculous not to. But the consequences of thinking and behaving in this way are far-reaching. Once we start worrying about what we will eat tomorrow, we start storing food, and we interfere with an ancient process. This process serves the centred, and not the linear, version of events. 'What we need will find us' is superseded by 'what we need must be engineered'. The former makes us vulnerable to a natural process that we destroyed during the Neolithic Revolution when agriculture took over from hunting. Our civilized minds have since lost the ability to appreciate how nature might provide for us without our intervention. These days, to rely on an impulsive nature alone would now have apocalyptic results. Our lives would become stressful and haphazard while we grab what we can and hope for the best.

However, in contrast to this anxiety, the *integrity principle* allows primitive people to live in a universe of order and control that *serves* nature. As a result, people find they have all that they need.

> "...the original affluent society was none other than the hunter's—in which all the people's material wants were easily satisfied." *Marshall Sahlins*

We tend to feel reassured by science's predictable and clockwork picture of life, and we think that nature is the one whose chaos needs taming. But according to the scientific laws of chaos, nature's non-linear system only appears chaotic because it cannot *accommodate errors*. This concurs with the primeval *integrity principle*, which states that we cannot break any primitive laws without landing ourselves with a different perception of existence. On the other hand, Newton's deterministic laws *can* accommodate errors as they apply to a purely linear system that allows errors to travel through time predictably. This enables us to manage them relatively easily. With regard to an impulsive and irrational nature, this is not the case. Nature's volatility cannot contain anomalies without them overrunning and ruining the system altogether. This is why nature appears unmanageable, and why it causes modern man so many problems. However, nature's inability to accept anomalies would not appear chaotic were we to exist *within* the system. Instead, we would experience law and order in the form of *spontaneous synchronicity*, such as we find in flocks of birds in flight, shoals of fish or hives of bees.

If we are one bird flying in a formation of many birds, such as Canada geese, we are not behaving randomly. We are part of a structured but instinctive routine where natural-law breakers would throw the flock into chaos. As natural humans, instinct, simplicity, and sensitivity would also guide us, as if through a dance or a geometric pattern, the design of which we would intuitively know. This is how primitive people are able to not care about whether they will eat tomorrow. It is this ancient instinct and natural connectivity that is now considered to be irrational and unreliable.

But we may find that as part of this primitive dance we would feel light-hearted and free. Our senses would reawaken and attune to nature. Perhaps we would find ourselves existing as an essential part of a simple universe, where time, space, geography, distance, and weight are not present, or at least unimportant. As a primitive species, we would not exist as aggressive consumers of the environment, but as an integral part of the natural world. We would provide a small but meaningful con-tribution to the vast diversity of life on Earth. This is a little of what life was like for our million-year-old ancient man.

CHAPTER 2

The Truth About Ritual

'All the world's a stage, and all the men and women players'
William Shakespeare

To have little or no impact on the land is true for most hunter-gatherers that exist in small numbers. This is due to the limits imposed by the natural productivity of the environment they inhabit and the fact that they do not work to overcome those limits, or assume to disregard them. For those who are profoundly primitive, this lightness that exists between earth and man extends beyond any physical impact towards a dreamlike quality of experience. Anthropologists and explorers have remarked on this quality over the centuries. This quality is not a vagueness or an emptiness. It manifests in the ease with which they interact with their surroundings, in the way they read and respond to their omens, and how they relate to everything in the atmosphere. Animism is the instinctive language of their primitive domain, and they speak it fluently.

Heavy duty

The Onge people are an isolated indigenous tribespeople of the Andaman and Nicobar Islands, situated in the Bay of Bengal in South East Asia. The DNA of the Onge people dates back at least 70,000 years, yet less than a hundred remain today. These people are renowned for avoiding the devastation of one of the most violent natural disasters in human history, what has come to be known as the Boxing Day tsunami. On 26 December 2004, a tsunami generated by a massive earthquake in the Indian Ocean hit the coasts of Indonesia, Sri Lanka, India, and Thailand killing an estimated 230,000 people. The Onge people avoided this deadly wave by interpreting omens from the sea, the birds, and the wind. They were able to run inland to high ground and to safety, where they lived on coconuts for a few weeks until it was safe to return. It was their integral relationship with the environment that enabled them to hear nature's warnings loud and clear. This story is a touching example of the gift of primitive simplicity.

Now contrast these tribes' skills in predicting the weather with modern forecasting abilities, or indeed our ability to set up a tsunami warning system in the Indian Ocean. To construct an infrastructure that could warn *us* of such a wall of water would involve masses of manpower, heavy machinery, sophisticated technology including weather satellites, and enormous financial investment. And even after all that it might not always work. The lightness of the tribespeople's intuition in contrast to the weight and complexity of our industry is the point here.

Anthropologists and others who spend any time with primitive tribes in isolation are often struck by how heavy and rigid the modern world seems on their return home. In civilized society, we are surrounded by hundreds of man-made items that we could never attempt to lift because of the great weight they possess—cars, buildings, lamp posts, cruise ships, aeroplanes, furniture, washing machines, ticket machines, petrol pumps, trucks. Everywhere there are gargantuan things that are busy serving modern humans and their lifestyles.

On the other hand, nothing heavy exists in the lives of primitive nomads. Their homes blow down in the wind, they sit on the ground, and their simple daily activities do not require lamp posts or washing machines. We might assume that this is common sense considering their transitional way of life. It is not practical for nomads to carry heavy objects around, so they do not accumulate any heavy objects. It is a simple equation. Accordingly, it would seem that we moderns who are no longer nomadic are free to make things as large and as heavy as we want, and to fill our houses and the whole world with them. But from a psychological perspective, this is not quite the whole story. The primitive nomadic lifestyle avoids accumulating stuff, *not* because they cannot carry it around, but because they do not have a mindset that is able to design or invent anything heavy. The lightness with which they perceive the world does not permit the generation of weight. It is their primitive psychology that keeps them clutter-free, not just the impracticality of having to move from camp to camp with loads of furniture and belongings. The weight contained in the *idea* of a cruise ship is equivalent to the physical weight it holds. For a primitive mind to create such a thing is incomprehensible, whether it is physical or imagined. (Within this scenario, there are other factors in conflict with a primitive mind, such as the *immodesty* of a cruise ship, which we will discuss later.)

The twentieth-century American sociologist Lewis Mumford, in his first book *The Story of Utopias*, refers to an *idolum*. According to Mumford, an *idolum* is a world of ideas that represents mankind's hidden inner world. It is a place where not just ideas but fantasies, longings, dreams, and philosophies reside and work to motivate the individual. He describes this secluded world as being as solid and as real as the physical world.

> '...this world of ideas—this idolum—is almost as sound, almost as real, almost as inescapable as the bricks of our house or the asphalt beneath our feet.'

Our interest in Mumford's *idolum* is two-fold. First, he identifies a world that we cannot see, but the existence of which we cannot deny because we all experience it. We know what it is to have a personal inner world that our desires, ambitions, and beliefs occupy. Second, he refers to these ideas as being just as solid as physical things because they are the driving force behind everything we do. They form the *intention* behind the action:

> 'An idea is a solid fact, a theory is a solid fact, a superstition is a solid fact as long as people continue to regulate their actions in terms of the idea, theory or superstition; and it is none the less solid because it is conveyed as an image or a breath of sound.'

This personal cauldron comprises all sorts of thoughts, convictions, and interpretations of the external world. It makes up who we are as individuals. It dictates to us what we do, how, and why. But however familiar this hidden world may seem to our minds, it is a truly modern phenomenon. The act of storing thoughts and feelings removes us from an integral relationship with our environment as we turn to face inward. Turning our focus away from the world outside in this way culminates in our view of it being obscured.

A screenshot of a document set within the document

It is like taking a screen capture of the document I am typing and inserting it as an object into the document that is in the capture. The document I am typing then becomes a feature contained within itself, existing as a self-perpetuating, inward-facing, two-dimensional image. This reduces the act to an object. It is no longer set within the circumstances of its original or true state. This screenshot is a representation of how our conscious minds internalize a free-flowing experience so that it becomes fixed. It has lost its connection with the elements that created it and has taken on a life of its own.

Primitive minds are distinctly different in the way they process thoughts and feelings. They do not internalize. An anthropologist friend of mine once tried to explain to a female elder of the Indian Apa Tani people about the Western idea of the 'inner child' as a term we use for storing emotional experiences from our past. On hearing the term 'inner' the woman looked puzzled. She started turning her head left and right, and looking behind her as if she expected to see someone standing there. After some confusion, it turned out that she could not conceive of 'inner' in relation to a person so she translated it into 'behind'. In tribal life, there is no well-defined individuality. Tribal people express all their thoughts, feelings, wants, and desires quite openly for the rest of the tribe to see—there is no *idolum*. The laws of animism also state that there is no in or out. There is no boundary between us and the environment, so the concept of using the inside of a person as a storage facility is a strange one. In the end, my friend explained it to her by using the image of a box to represent the person, and then having something inside the box that related to the past. She responded with horror and said it sounded ghostly. Someone with an 'inner child' must be possessed. As opposed to coming from the 'inside', primitive people are more likely to see emotional influences such as these as 'attaching' to you. Once they are 'in' they have taken you over, and you would need treatment from the tribe's medicine person or even excluding from the tribe altogether. For a primitive mind, these hidden, internal realms are dangerous places in which shadows can hide. These shadows are influences that bring unwanted sickness and conflict to the group and disrupt the domestic harmony that resides at the heart of tribal life.

Primitive individuals, while lacking this inner world which we are so familiar with, appear to have more of a hidden *outer* world. What motivates and drives them is on display, larger than life, in their environment. They communicate with the world in a way that we are unable to see, hear or understand. This animistic language is not a philosophy or religion with no common foundation. Nor does it only apply to certain individuals. For these people, it is simply the state of the world as they find it, albeit invisible to our eyes and ears. As we stand upon the border of these two worlds, we find they are mutually exclusive. While we will never have access to their animistic otherworld, they will never penetrate our consciousness within.

> 'I could never have proved to the Pirahãs that the beach was empty. Nor could they have convinced me that there was anything, much less a spirit, on it.' *Daniel Everett, Don't Sleep There Are Snakes*

The heaviness we live with today—inside and out—as opposed to this lightness and expressiveness is the manifestation of the *idea* of weight that we have given weight to. We could say that the physical weight we experience only exists because we focus on that idea—the idea that weight exists—and so, for us, it does. In a primitive dimension, *values* replace *weight* because the focus is on *relationship*. Therefore, weight cannot take part unless we are weighing values.

The invention of thought control

For a primitive mind, therefore, a clear intention is at the heart of every action. There is no division between the two; there is no duality. There is no in or out—intention *is* action. If someone in your tribe feels jealous they will act out that jealousy, if they feel love they will act out love, if they need to go hunting they will go hunting, and so on. This is the basis of unconscious behaviour in animals and primitive humans.

If we consider our more familiar process of desire *followed by* thought *followed by* action, we can see how by separating these elements, we create a sequential event that can only exist within our modern linear framework. As we enact this sequence, we create events with spaces in between, spaces that are *filled with time*. These spaces—albeit hardly noticeable—are pivotal to the way modern society has evolved. They enable the conscious control of our thoughts and behaviour by creating opportunities to alter the intention before it becomes an action. The result: we can have an action that appears to be *unintentional*. And so, the capacity for social deceit is born. Now, we have a process with which we can choose to conceal or disguise what we think and feel by acting out something to the contrary. For truly primitive people, their psychology makes this impossible for them to do. This is not because they are 'good', but because their spontaneous emotionality prevents them from separating their drive from their behaviour. In other words, they are unable to act unintentionally.

To carry this further, our dualistic world starts to consist of a physical version on the outside and a conscious mental version on the inside. These two distinct interpretations of the environment define the boundary between inside and outside. They become separated from each other, and the process is irreversible. It is at this point that the natural world shuts us out, and we lose the ability to communicate with it. Tribal people who are animists have not made this separation. Their intention is still their action. Their behaviour and what drives their behaviour are the same.

The next stage in this process is that the version of a situation that occupies each of our minds starts to become different from one another. Personal interpretation means there are millions of individualized renderings of life and the world in existence. Each version that is inside each mind is distinct from every other. Except, each one is just as real to each of those minds as the one world outside is. This diversity in personal interpretations and the complete chaos it causes is what drives us to obsessively define and measure the physical world. It has become the only version of events that we can agree on. Out of the chaos, we must establish order of some kind. Our personal *idolums* prevent us from agreeing on fundamental issues that are important to us, such as suitable codes of conduct, social values or how to look after the environment. But we are able to agree on how many miles there are across France or how many millimetres there are across a butterfly's wing. This is the moment that the collective human experience arrives in the physical world, and it becomes unquestionably real. The trouble is, we now have to act out these measurements. We have no option but to travel the miles across France and the millimetres across the butterfly's wing simply because we have created them. Our intent alone is no longer able to draw us to the experience without the accompanying 'bits in between'. This three-dimensional universal agreement is the price we have to pay for selfhood.

This method of separating intention from action is fundamental to modern thought processes. Consciousness allows us to set store by the physical action (including what we say) without having an understanding of what lies behind it. As Arthur Schopenhauer pointed out in his essay *On the Freedom of Will* in the nineteenth century, 'Man can do what he wills but he cannot will what he wills'—that is to say, we cannot falsify our intention. But, now we have separated it from our behaviour we can *disguise* it by falsifying our action, so the two no longer match up. The upshot of this is that the physical act is all we focus on. Whatever thoughts and feelings motivate it have ended up in the foggy realms of personal opinion. Social ambiguity like this is dangerous for any community because it provides a hiding place for liars, upstarts, and bullies.

Spoken language has also developed a considerable authority in modern social dynamics. We find ourselves only focusing on what people are saying while their subtler body language and facial expressions might be communicating something to the contrary. When two people meet and have a conversation, they exchange a wealth of experience and information that has little to do with the words they are sharing. True intentions can remain under the carpet; 'we speak with fork tongue', as some natives might say. Human interaction has become steeped in mind games. Our motives have become masked, and emotional engineering is commonplace. Personalized methods of interpretation and judgement are the only tools we have to decide what is legitimate and what is not. This is something that is becoming ever more difficult to do with any clarity.

This uncomfortable world of psychological hide and seek is now deeply rooted in our social fabric, from our families to our politics. The separation of intention from action is a key component of this story about perceived realities. Intentionality is a vast, no-nonsense but invisible force of nature. It drives the wind and makes acorns grow into oak trees. It causes the rain to fall, and it is what brings out the sun from behind a cloud to form a rainbow. And despite our behaviour to the contrary, human beings are not exempt. Intention is at the heart of all life in the natural world and an enigma that science still struggles to understand:

> 'The simple statement "a drop falls off the tap" is accomplished by way of an amazingly complex and surprising sequence of transitions. We do not yet know *why* those transitions derive from the laws of fluid flow, although we have…evidence that they do.' Ian Stewart, *Nature's Numbers*

There are various cultural interpretations of this intentionality, or natural drive: *Qi* (or *Chi*) in traditional Chinese, *Prana* in Hindu, *Lung* in Tibetan Buddhism, and *Mana* in Polynesian, Melanesian and Hawaiian cultures. In the West, it was once known as a *vital energy* which was associated with the soul. All refer to a natural life force that has its root in a supernatural otherworld. I tend to avoid these terms due to their religious and new-age associations. Instead, I refer to 'intention' as much as possible because it relates more aptly to a primitive lifeworld. I even invent my own name for this vitality towards the end of the book.

The loss of ritual

Closely related to the neat and clean intention of a primitive mind is the art of primitive ritual. Ritualistic patterns of behaviour govern the lightweight everyday world of tribal people. These rituals help to keep the intention and the action we have just talked about firmly together.

Mainstream texts refer to ritual acts carried out by primitive people as *performances* that express important aspects—often spiritual ones—within their lives. Tribal people today who perform rituals are thought to demonstrate a certain level of creative sophistication. Prehistorians pinpoint the emergence of this behaviour in significant evolutionary terms to about 50,000 BCE. Ceremonial rituals that appeared around this time, such as burial rituals and art, are evidence that mankind was developing away from the unconscious animal into a being who could observe and then repeat that observation as a meaningful statement. But, before people started to change in this way, ritual would have been a vital part of life in a distinctly different way.

Ritual behaviour in very early humans would have been as we see it in animals: unconscious repetitive acts according to the laws and behavioural patterns of one's species. Biologists describe this repetitive behaviour as innate responses to biological cues. As psychologists, we call it ritual. The act of ritual is not ceremonial or formal amongst truly primitive people. It is an instinctive pattern of activities or events, which allow them to take part in the practical mechanics of life as much as they ever should. It prevents them from taking their behaviour any further. It is the only way that unconscious animals can plan for the future because it *limits* their activities according to their species. If their behaviour is not ritualized, the future becomes chaotic because it is limit*less*. Life starts to develop and change ad infinitum, and no longer according to any natural laws.

When ritual is in its most primitive form, it is not planned or arranged. Organized performances, such as the Native American Ghost Dance or the African Bushmen's Healing Ritual, have developed out of social difficulties. They do not relate to the everyday activities of the people. These are events triggered by social anxiety, yet we would still consider them to be primitive acts. The Ghost Dance, like some other tribal trance-like rituals, was a desperate performance to put right something in the lives of natives that had gone seriously wrong. The Sioux and other plains tribes hoped it would '...lead to the destruction of the whites, the resurrection of ancestors, and a nativist return to the pure old ways of the tribes' (Page 2003). For now, we need to separate unconscious primitive ritual behaviour from this type of performance that evolved as a result of social interference and disturbance.

We find primitive ritual behaviour in the everyday activities of tribal people. These activities are often repetitive and are bound by the social values that the tribe agrees on. The ritualistic or repetitive aspect of the behaviour ensures everyone knows what to do and how to do it. Hunting is a ritual, sweeping the hut is a ritual, washing is a ritual, cooking is a ritual. Daily tasks are always performed in a similar way, perhaps in a certain order or while singing a specific song. There may be particular rules to obey, such as no men at the birth of a baby or not eating after sundown. Tribal people do not enact these events in a ceremonial way. They do not make spells or recite incantations. Their rituals are their behaviour, just as their intentions are their actions. It is a simple and down-to-earth format that they follow using their instincts.

True ritual plays a significant role in the life of our ancient man. It acts as an anchor: the simple patterns that he acts out prevent him uncoupling from his place within his tribe and the environment. The result of having a behavioural framework like this in place is that social change becomes immensely difficult to initiate.

We also witness this behaviour in animals and birds. A buzzard and her offspring perform an elegant dance in the late summer when the time is right for the youngster to leave his parents' side. Together they dance figures of eight, high on the warm thermals, mum making her haunting call and mobbing the teenager now and again as if to say 'off you go'. Dad is nearby watching as they act out what their ancestors have acted out for hundreds of thousands of years. Their intention becomes the dance, and that is the ritual. Some people might look on at this ritual and see a parent evicting a child from the family home. Others may see a behavioural response to a biological cue. But as we observe the patterns and listen to their calls, we might recognize remarkable order and natural law in the form of instinctive behaviour, expressed in a beautiful, ritualized dance.

What is real?

Any good actor in a play by William Shakespeare will know that faking it on stage is something the playwright himself has made very difficult to do. Yet most non-actors will say that acting is all about faking. In actual fact, when we are on stage, our intent is far more difficult to disguise than when we are in a social situation that we would consider to be real life. Bad actors become awkward as they try to hide misplaced intentions or emotions that are stuck. Perhaps they feel nervous, self-conscious, or have a fear of doing it 'wrong', but the results can be agonizing to watch. However, in an everyday social setting, conscious control of our outward expression is far easier to manage and our feelings easier to conceal, because they are not under such intense scrutiny. Shakespeare's writing demands that his actors have no controls of this kind due to the broad spectrum of feelings they are required to express throughout his plays. As a result, the audience travels with the actors through the many realms of human emotion in a ritualistic fashion, just like the primitive buzzards.

Another compelling factor relating to ritualistic behaviour is the attention to what I call 'loophole events'. This term refers to the ritual as a pre-emptive act that works to cancel out any potential bad luck or negative influence that might be trying to find us. If we are living a primitive life with a primitive mind, then we are inherently part of an unconscious integrity that is resistant to negative influence. There is no magical force field at work here. It is the rituals we act out that address any potential security breaches or loopholes. These loopholes involve factors such as sickness, jealousy or conflict within the tribe, which can flare up at any moment and disrupt everyone. To ensure none of these scenarios ambush us out of the blue, we act out the scenarios before they happen. The idea is that we will not have to it act out 'for real' if we act it out ritually first. This is the principle at the heart of this design. It keeps everyday routines predictable and manageable.

In the modern world, we have come to expect the unexpected and so accommodate the pressure and anxiety that accompany random events that occur at any moment. We accept that life will deal us a blow here and there. On the other hand, our ancient man would not survive such an affront. The strain and insecurity it would cause would damage the intuitive qualities that allow him to live in harmony with his tribe and the natural world. As it is, while he continues with the rituals and if he does not change according to primitive law, his life remains stable and his familiar reality intact.

How authentic or not human behaviour is according to ritual and routine presents us with a paradox. We view our modern actions and experiences as so *real* and ritual or acting so *unreal* that our patterns of behaviour, which are now driven by free will and individuality, have become muddled and erratic. Ritual is no longer the basis for our everyday lives. We are making it up as we go along. The result of this improvisation is that personal loopholes appear that bring bad luck. Predicaments arise out of the blue such as accidents, illnesses or work-related scenarios such as redundancies. We end up feeling buffeted around by situations that appear to be out of our control.

Blackbird knows about loopholes. He sings his rich song at dawn and he will always do so during the months of the year that he sings. He also protests at dusk. As the sun goes down he 'snips' like scissors to show his disapproval to the oncoming darkness. These are examples of simple repetitive rituals that contribute to the sun coming up and going down each day. A modern civilized mind would consider this a pointless exercise as we know that the sun will come up and go down anyway. But in the unconscious, animistic dimension the blackbird is living in, every aspect—animal, bird, plant, rock, water—plays a part in the smooth running of the environment. We also know this to be the case in the physical world. In terms of ecosystems, organisms and their environments are also entwined in an intricate relationship of interdependence. And so it is with ritual. How do we know that should all the blackbirds cease singing the sun would not stop rising, at least for them? The *integrity principle* and their species-specific rituals keep these birds free from loopholes and immune to the chaos of a life with no limits. Only when we have removed ourselves from that integrity do we consider it unnecessary to make a contribution to the upkeep of our environment in this symbolic way. For the animals that we are, nature has merely become a picturesque backdrop to something far more important and complicated.

> 'The blackbird did not question his personal rights to the land, for he was part of the land, as necessary to the earth as a small sentence may be to a book whose text depends upon every single word for its completeness;' *Patrick Jasper Lee, We*

Borrow the Earth: An Intimate Portrait of the Gypsy Folk Tradition and Culture

We find remnants of these loophole rituals in modern human life too. Wishing an actor good luck by telling him to 'break a leg' before going on stage is an example. The traditional Romani Gypsy ritual where everyone 'pretends' to have a brawl at a wedding or funeral is another. I was once fortunate enough to attend such a wedding. After the ceremony and before the reception began, the bride suddenly picked on one of the guests. Within minutes, both families were arguing, shouting, and pushing each other around. After a while, we ran out of steam and fell about laughing. It was exhilarating and a lot of fun.

While this does not sound very dignified, there are a few subtle, psychological advantages to a performance such as this, which I realized afterwards. First, getting married can be considerably stressful. The mock fight relieved the wedding party of any strain that might have built up over the previous few hours or days, by acting out a possible result of that strain before it happened *for real.* Then we were free to go on and enjoy the party that followed without carrying it all along with us. Most people underestimate the sort of strain we are talking about here. It is an invisible threat to the collective, a social pressure cooker that we tend to ignore. It bubbles menacingly under the surface of social occasions and erupts when it is most inconvenient and always when we are unprepared. But, if we have already enacted this dangerous scenario as a ritual, it is less likely to occur out of the blue later on. Second, if any unsavoury feelings such as resentment or jealousy are lurking among the people acting out the fight, the ritual will expose them, just as it exposes the actors in a Shakespeare play. Although we *think* we are pretending, we cannot pretend if we are doing it for real. As if we are individuals in a tribe, the ritual exposes our intentions to the elements for everyone to see. It is then that we are required to deal with them so that life can go back to normal once again.

Loophole ritual behaviour is also evident in some of the warriorship or mock combat rituals that we find in traditional cultures from around the world. Examples of these rituals include the low contact martial arts from the Far East, the Brazilian Capoeira, and the Maori Hukka. These combat rituals or dances express the natural qualities that warriors would have worked to earn, such as courage, fierceness, and precision. As rituals, these performances have nothing to do with actual fighting. Like rutting stags, they attend to a loophole by expressing conflict under controlled conditions and *before* any real conflict arises. In fact, it would have been the closest primitive ancient people got to an actual fight. Our axeman may have been such a warrior, who ritualized his intention to protect his clan and to stand up for the principles by which they lived their peaceful lives. He probably never imagined that one day people would be acting out that intention *for real*.

Symbolism and patterns

Within both the realm of dreams and the realm of ritual, there is symbolism. Symbolism is the visible manifestation of an animistic otherworld. Omens are symbols that primitive minds interpret as messages. Nothing is ever by chance in a primitive

world, which is the point and art of ritual that we have established. When we ritualize our behaviour, life remains simple
and the same. Unscheduled incidents cannot threaten what is
usual within the tribe. Therefore, when something out of the
ordinary does happen, it stands out loud and clear, and everyone immediately looks for an interpretation of what it means.
A flock of birds flying in an unusual formation or an animal
crossing the path in a certain direction, a sudden gust of wind
or dark clouds on the horizon, a pod of whales dying on a
beach—these are all events that would scream messages and intent to a primitive mind. That mind would then relate those
messages to what is happening in their tribe and the rest of the
environment.

The word inauguration comes from the Latin *inaugurare*, 'to
take omens from the flight of birds'. An inauguration is a formal
ceremony that inducts a new official into office or marks the
beginning of a new project or organization. It dates back to at
least the sixteenth century. At the ceremony, those present
would look to the sky for signs from the birds with which they
could forecast the providence of the leader's term in office or
the new project's success. Imagine the next U.S. president at
their inauguration, asking her advisors, 'What do the birds say?'
Of course, for an accurate answer she would need to have a true
native at her side. But the etymology of this word shows us how
recently the symbolic otherworld was a meaningful influence
in people's lives.

An example of how symbolic imagery continues to penetrate our world from the invisible otherworld occurred last
night in my kitchen. While my husband Jasper was cooking

dinner, our eight-year-old son pointed to the perfect image of a hand that had appeared as a large shadow on the wall. It was cast by a light shining through a knife block on the worktop. We discussed how a prehistoric mind would see the image of the hand coming through from the otherworld, probably belonging to a spirit. The hand would be an omen giving us a message, but one that is difficult to decipher from the perspective of our modern kitchen and our modern psychologies. In a primitive world, we would not acknowledge the physical source of the image, namely the knife block and the light: we would consider it irrelevant, even if we could be that objective. Whose hand it is and what it represents are all that matter. Rational explanations are of no consequence.

Our dreams are full of symbolism. While we sleep, our minds produce images that we could translate in a similar way to omens. Furthermore, we do not experience all the 'bits in between' that we inherit from linear time. In a dream, we would not wait for the kettle to boil or drive miles to the shopping centre. We would drink the tea or be in the shop, cutting directly to the point of action. Our memory is the same. It is sketchy and discriminatory according to relevance and impact, with the mundane moments evaporating away. But we do not consider memories to consist of symbols, only what we would consider to be facts. From a primitive point of view, memory is a strange mental phenomenon. It is a mechanism that supports our modern 3D time and space agreement, and it holds a powerful relevance in our lives. Consciousness and memory amount to a mind full of measured dreams splintered by time. Memories are recorded moments that repeat randomly as a string of familiar images, like a necklace of precious jewels hidden in a box. These recordings lie dormant within our personal *idolums,* where the calendar and the clock, our diaries and photographs sustain them. They require the capacity for mental storage, and the primitive lack of storage indicates that memory is a phenomenon peculiar to civilized minds.

From dreams to discoveries

Animism, symbolism, and a dreamlike perception cannot flourish within a linear framework of experience. They thrive within a framework far more characteristic of the centred sphere that we met in the last chapter. Let us use that metaphor again. Imagine that our perceived universe is set within the sphere and now imagine that the sphere is made of bread dough. What would happen if we pulled on the dough and stretched it out into a single string? The present, which we permanently occupy, would expand in a single direction and determine every single period of time throughout history and the future. The dinosaurs would suddenly die out 65 million years ago. The big bang would appear as the universe's momentous beginning, and the end—the big crunch—would become an inevitable but unknown event that we cannot predict because it remains out of sight. The universe would exist in a line, with each event that occurs appearing in a sequence one after the other. We would also have to suffer the incredibly boring 'bits in between' that lead from one experience or event to another. Like washing drying on the line in our garden, there is always something between one item and the next, but it is only a bit of the washing line, nothing more. These are the deleted scenes where we drive to the shops or wait for the bus to arrive or the program to load. We no longer have access to all the relevant moments at once as they are now distributed throughout the string as links in a chain.

Looking at sequence in this way helps us to make sense of the modern human obsession with discovery. As we travel along the string of dough, we encounter new ideas. We progress concepts we have already unearthed; developments evolve one step at a time. But the things we discover about life, ourselves, and the universe are not really new. They are links in the chain that we could not see because linearity had obscured them. Modern humans can only be discoverers and inventors, builders and developers, because of this linearity. Without it, there would be nothing to discover. And so, we surrender to the evolutionary process where one finding must lead to another and another. That being the case, the principles of how the universe works *without* linearity must reside within each link of the chain we travel along. They would be immediately available to us if we could only extract that staunch sense of mileage from our experience and perception of the world.

Within the non-linearity of the primitive world, we may find that the principles of all sorts of ideas and technologies are available, including ideas, perceptions, and periods of time *we* are yet to discover. In this place, the beginning and the end of the world exist together as a standard paradigm. Scientific and mathematical principles occur in a complete state and not in a mode of constant unveiling and innovation. Nature wields the power of the golden ratio, the square root of two, and pi continuously. These are the components of the primeval world of our ancient man, yet within his world, they are not fixed objects in their own right. They are part of a vast framework of processes which are not measured or observed, they are not thingified. There they remain in their original dreamlike form, suggesting that even an object as bold and defiant as an Egyptian pyramid should be merely an image that could come and go. It should not be an indestructible mountain of weight stuck fast in linear time.

Considering this perspective, a technology that we have long forgotten and not yet rediscovered may be responsible for building the Great Pyramids and other ancient monuments. It could be a hidden link in the modern chain of discovery and time, which is accessible at any moment in our forbidden, primeval world. Bearing in mind the people who built these structures lived *before* the arrow of time was established, and before the structure of nature had been thingified, this is a possibility. We explore megalithic architecture in more detail in Chapter 10—*Monumental Collapse*. But before we can understand the extraordinary technology people had at their disposal during the Neolithic and Bronze Ages, we need to identify the other vital principles that make up the foundation of our forbidden dimension. The world we have uncovered thus far is built from qualities such as light-hearted simplicity, animism and intentionality, non-linearity, the inability to change, and instinctive ritualized behaviour. We are glimpsing a perceived reality that is robust, harmonious, and sustainable. But this is just the tip of the iceberg.

CHAPTER 3

Life in the Penal Colony

'The kumara [sweet potato] does not say how sweet he is.'
Maori proverb

The practice of ostracism plays an important role in our story about the prehistoric world. It is a substantial primitive law that our ancient man knows well. Today, we find primitive tribes, herd animals, and insects practising ostracism—groups whose social structures are threatened with disruption from upstarts and rogue individuals. Ostracism as a tool for social control fits with the tribal social framework as it attacks the fundamental need to belong within that framework. A truly primitive clan is a remarkable feat of social engineering. Only in the last 10,000 years have we seen the breakdown of its subtle arrangement into complex societies composed of political hierarchies, irreconcilable codes of conduct and religious ideals. The corruption of the process of ostracism has played a part in that breakdown, and this is what we are exploring in this chapter.

A democratic process

The word ostracism comes from the Greek noun *ostrakon*. It refers to a broken potsherd the ancient Athenians used to cast a vote. They used this vote to exile an individual from the city for a period of time. In around 500 BCE, the Greeks introduced this process to alleviate political clashes or tyrannical uprisings simply by having the person at the root of the problem removed. This individual would not lose any social status nor have their belongings confiscated. On their return to the city (after a period of up to ten years) they would endure no stigma—they could go about their business as if nothing had ever happened. There was no formal judicial procedure, no charge or mention of an offence, no jury, and no invitation to explain. It was a simple vote by the people to have an individual, notably one who was getting too big for their boots, removed for the sake of the rest of the city, no questions asked. It was an orderly affair and occurred once a year. The Athenian citizens assembled in the Agora and wrote on their *ostrakon* the name of the person they would like to remove. They banished the one with the most votes and gave them ten days to get their affairs in order before they left.

One reason why this ancient Athenian practice is so compelling is that running alongside it was the birth of our modern justice system. This was a very different affair: the specific complaint by an individual and the subsequent prosecution, defence, trial, and judgement of the accused. Punishment was usually death, even for minor offences. Still, the ancient Greeks invented the basis of the system we have today: an elite minority in society decides the fate of an individual accused of breaking a law that another elite minority has determined. But the process of ostracism demonstrated the Athenians' power as a *majority* of equals to remove an individual whose personal power was a threat to the collective. This 'reverse dominance hierarchy' (Boehm 2001), where the powerful and dominant individual is placed at the bottom and not at the top, is not new. It is the social foundation of egalitarian hunter-gatherer tribes and, therefore, ancient human life. For hundreds of thousands, maybe millions, of years, tribal people exercised control of upstarts and bullies in this way.

One might wonder how these two systems could coexist in Ancient Greece with such obvious disparities, so it will not be a surprise to find out that they did not for long. The Athenians viewed their employment of ostracism as a democratic process. But in truth, it was a simple tribal principle that they returned to as problems of personal power amongst political individuals escalated. Primitive ostracism is a method that tribal people continue to use today to manage disruptive individuals in their communities, although the process is less formal. These tribes know that to entertain traits such as arrogance, selfishness, greed, or intimidation, can lead to dire consequences. Demonstrations of traits like these threaten the social integrity of the tribe. They must be stopped before they can develop—pre-emption is critical for the survival of the group. The egalitarian ethos is unable to accommodate personal attitudes that might upset the harmonious dynamic of daily life.

However, in ancient Athens where sharing and equality were not founding notions of the culture, the simple process of ostracism struggled with the intricacies of their politics and social relationships. They abandoned it amid fears of vote rigging and corruption in 417 BCE.

Feelings matter

Primitive ostracism addresses the violation of an established tribal principle or value by an individual. This violation can manifest in many ways, perhaps as a minor display of disrespect, rudeness or laziness, or something more disruptive such as theft or even sorcery. As a result, the individual will find themselves placed on the outside of their tribe, excluded from the normal comforting world they know. Imagine, on a cold, dark night your family throws you out of your comfy, warm house and slams the door behind you. And you cannot just put your key in the door and walk defiantly back in, sleeves rolled and ready for an argument. You must wait for your family to open the door and allow you back in. Primitive ostracism is about learning and expressing the values that the tribe share. It is not a tit-for-tat argument about what is right or wrong. If we do not blend with those values, then we are a liability. We will find ourselves placed on the outside until the tribe considers us safe to have around.

Ostracism in primitive terms does not always occur in a physical sense. Even within our modern lives we know it is possible to feel ostracized in a room full of people or a playground full of children. There are subtle levels to this process, often invisible to the observer, which places the individual in a 'space'. We experience that space as an agonizing isolation, regardless of whether we are in physical contact with people or not. The ostracized space is uncomfortable. Within it we can feel humiliated, fearful, vulnerable, anxious or depressed. It is interesting to note that even a brief spell of ostracism activates the anterior cingulate cortex—the part of the brain that detects pain (Williams 2001).

> 'To not perceive being ignored and excluded would be similar to not perceiving the pain of fire...enduring it without responding would only ensure its devastating effects.' *Kipling D Williams, Ostracism: The Power of Silence*

The result of ostracism should be that the individual searches for the qualities they have misplaced, such as modesty or good manners. Only then will the tribe allow them to return to their normal life, relieved of the discomfort that exclusion had imposed upon them. No one should dwell or wallow. Self-pity—a rare trait in primitive people—only furthers the distance between where we are and where we should be according to our tribe.

In the primitive dimension, exclusion can happen in a second. It does not occur in varying degrees but as an instantaneous, inevitable result of an expression or behaviour. We find ourselves on the outside with noses pressed against the window. Linear time is not present in this place and so is not part of the process. Shunned and ignored, we are obligated to embark on a journey in search of realizations about what we have done and inspiration for what we need to do to put things right. This journey resembles a cycle or a loop that will bring us back to ourselves, but perhaps wiser and a little more mature. It should not be a path that leads somewhere new, or worse, nowhere at all. This is where we find the origins of distance and travel. Distance equals separation. In a primitive world, people do not define separation in terms of physical miles or kilometres across the planet, but in how far we have drifted from our normal role and place within the tribe. The point of ostracism is that we return to our original selves. In this way, it links to our million-year-old man and the principle of not changing. Enlightened, reformed, and relieved the tribe embraces us back, and life is as it should be once again.

Christopher Boehm, in his book *The Hierarchy in the Forest: The Evolution of Egalitarian Behavior,* identifies three main deviants who threaten tribal society: upstarts, bullies, and free-riders, all of whom are usually male. In hunting and foraging bands, people's lives are based on principles of cooperation and sharing, so conflict is usually easy to resolve. However, if a conflict gets particularly heated or if someone repeatedly deviates from the social norm, exclusion will come into play. This is so that the discomfort placed on the majority is handed back to the individual. They are forced to take responsibility for their behaviour. It is a neat and tidy process.

When we employ ostracism in a social situation, it is the isolation that acts as the ruling force. It is an immense shock to the system, and this is particularly so when you live tribally. Isolating the individual deprives them of the basic necessities of life such as food and shelter. It also protects the rest of the tribe from their behaviour. As well, it provides a psychological 'place' within which they have room to recognize and accept their situation and then work to put it right. This place is not geographical but somewhere we find ourselves dealing with the inevitable consequences of our actions. It is the only place in a primitive dimension where thoughts and feelings such as those that led to our exclusion are able to reside. But it is not *inside* our minds because primitive people have no inside. It is like being imprisoned in an invisible room with no door. We will only find that door and open it when we change our attitude. If we do nothing, we will probably die.

Many people see ostracism as a painful social punishment that can have long-lasting psychological effects on its targets. However, from within the primitive social design, it illustrates how natural law provides an opportunity for upstarts to redeem themselves when they misbehave. But such forgiveness is strictly conditional. We must make amends and learn from the error of our ways if we want the clan to accept us back. Humans should not be able to survive the fatal isolation of an ostracized existence. This is nature's way of keeping her perfect world intact.

There are an awful lot of factors that have to be right for this to work as it once did. Ancient social life was an efficient and successful business, and the lack of hierarchy that spreads the balance of power throughout the tribe is a vital factor contributing to this. The primitive tribal ethos puts authority with the whole rather than with a selection of exclusive individuals. This structure inspires everyone in the tribe to contribute to the smooth running of daily life simply because everyone else is doing it.

> 'Firstly, it is not individuals but collectives that impose obligations of exchange and contract upon each other...In particular these exchanges are an act of politeness...in which the passing on of wealth is only one feature of a much more general and enduring contract.' *Marcel Mauss, The Gift: The Form and Reason for Exchange in Archaic Societies*

In a more authoritarian hierarchy that has an individual at the top telling everyone else what to do, dictation becomes the operative form of control. Guaranteed, the unpleasant face of resentment will quickly rise up in those who are on the receiving end. This is a dangerous scenario for a tribal community. Inequality is notorious for sowing the seeds of resentment and indignation. Allowing such bad feeling free rein within individuals could be lethal for any community, not just primitive ones. The success of an egalitarian society that is dependent on cooperation and sharing to survive relies on the complete absence of these feelings. So, it makes sense that tribal society has a structure that does not engineer them in the first place.

How dare you!

Unfortunately, in modern society feelings of resentment are commonplace. We know what it is like to feel bitter, bear a grudge or feel hard done by—uncomfortable to say the least. Expressing feelings like these can be an ugly business and will be a performance that is unlikely to make us any friends, particularly ones in high places. For this reason, it is often the case that we suppress these feelings, banishing them to our inner worlds where we try to justify them or simply disregard them altogether. But they do not go away. There they will stagnate, and if we ignore them or indeed nurture them, we can end up with some unpleasant psychological consequences, such as personality disorders and neuroses. In primitive terms, we can only rectify the situation by relinquishing what is inappropriate according to the laws of our tribe. With no inner world in which to hide them and no hierarchy with which to generate them, negative intentions cannot take hold. That is the whole point of this exquisite design.

It is when resentment does become tolerable within the sanctuary of daily social life that true primitive ostracism will never work. Then we find ourselves in some very hot water indeed. Banishment is not the shock to the system that it should be once people become accustomed to living with such discomfort. In fact, it could make the situation a whole lot worse. There is a danger that an individual could start up a completely new life in their isolated world. This new life would be founded on that same resentment and perhaps a few other unpleasant ingredients such as pride, stubbornness, irritation, single-mindedness, and determination. Should this happen, they would create an entirely new dimension of perception and understanding. Humans that are thereafter born into such a world would have a social foundation constructed from these properties. Cooperation, teamwork, participation, and humility would no longer underpin their codes of conduct. Instead, traits that would have primitive people ostracized will be intrinsic to their existence. And so, the 'penal colony' is born.

It is my view that the colonization of the ostracized mindspace in this way is at the heart of many of our current social and psychological difficulties. It is a phenomenon we will refer to throughout the book. The ostracized dimension is the only place that can accommodate the negative intentions and emotions we have identified. These intentions do not exist in the interdependent world of primeval nature *unless we ritualize them*. We have to think about this dimension as a perceived place that exists outside the psychological framework of a primitive mind. It is not somewhere geographical. It is as if a switch is flicked when we release these traits into the atmosphere, we are propelled to this place and left floundering. Then, inspired by our need to belong and according to the primitive laws of survival, we learn our lessons—*we are initiated*—and we return home. Setting up camp in the place of exclusion was certainly not a factor in the original design.

Staying in with the in-crowd

Ostracism's greatest power is as a deterrent. In modern society, we know how uncomfortable it feels to be singled out, excluded or ignored. We go to great lengths to fit in, whether it is with the whole of society, family, friends or the in-crowd. A simple social experiment on TV a few years ago demonstrated this point. It involved nine people in a room together, eight actors and one unknowing guinea pig. The nine were sat at a large table together completing application forms for a job. There were two doors in the room that they could clearly see. Underneath one of the doors smoke slowly emitted to suggest that the building was on fire. The actors pretended to be so absorbed by their form-filling that they did not notice the smoke. When the non-actor noticed it, four out of five times, they looked at the others who were not reacting and went back to their form. Only on one occasion did the guinea pig have the wherewithal to mention that the building might be on fire, and in the end got up and left.

Considering this was a life-threatening situation, the results of this experiment are quite mind-boggling. It illustrates our desperate need for anonymity and acceptance within a group, and in modern society, this need becomes a problem. Parents, teachers, sergeants, employers, religious and political leaders all exploit our willingness to conform, reject responsibility, and even tolerate physical suffering in order to *belong*. Perhaps you think you would be one of those who would act when no one else does, thereby saving your fellow form-fillers from burning to death. But the truth is 'heroes' are not the norm. They are deviants (Zimbardo 2008), non-conformists, and troublemakers, who will risk exclusion for what they believe is right. The rest of us conform because we need to belong to the group to survive. It is instinctive and fundamentally human. Kipling D Williams' book *Ostracism: The Power of Silence* is a rare study of the psychological effects of ostracism, and he echoes the conclusion of the TV experiment:

> '...men would change their perception of an unmistakably correct judgment about the length of a line simply to conform to the opinions of the unanimous majority of peers...'

In his book, Williams examines accounts from hundreds of people who have experienced social exclusion of some kind. From those accounts, we can conclude that our need to belong is alive and well, and so ostracism continues to thrive. But the nature of its employment has changed. In our society, we snub our friends, give work colleagues the cold shoulder, and ignore loved ones after an argument. These are all tactics of modern social warfare and very different from the primitive exclusion of upstarts and troublemakers. Sometimes subtle and even petty, these tactics in the wrong hands can be psychologically damaging and painful. Suffice to say, outside the management of a primitive group ostracism can be abusive, but within it, important values and principles are upheld. These principles are not a matter of opinion. They are the laws of the tribe that in turn keep people integral to the natural world. If we break them, if we start to lose ourselves in something personal, then we are no longer part of the social anatomy of our tribe. Therefore, we must be existing in a place with a different anatomy: ignorance can only exist in the place of ignorance.

Williams points out that the process of ostracism and its effects are rooted in the elementary or primitive layers of human psychology. He says that ostracism attacks four fundamental human needs:

> 'Our sense of belonging is severed; the control we desire between our actions and outcomes is uncoupled; our self-esteem is shaken by feelings of shame, guilt or inferiority; and we feel like a ghost, observing what life would be like if we didn't exist.'

We could rewrite this sentence in the order in which the experience occurs: I have tried to exercise control, and so I am ostracized; my sense of belonging is severed, my self-esteem is shaken by shame and guilt, and I feel like I don't exist. Now imagine we live in a primitive world where time is condensed, and experience is not sequential. There, the sentence would become 'my need for control means I do not exist' or 'my arrogance means I do not exist'—the cause and effect are bound together without the sequence of events in between. In primitive terms, it is not our exclusion that makes us feel like we do not exist. It is the need for control, the selfishness or whatever negative intentions we expressed that led to our exclusion. In this way, the primitive world is direct. If our intentions are offensive, we will reap the consequences, and *we do not resent the process* that leads us back to our tribe. In contrast, the modern world has created a situation where reaping the consequences of our actions may not even happen. The behaviour in question is now a matter of opinion that we can argue about. Simply identifying our intentions has become an impossible task. We also get lost in the process; we become stuck in the 'and' between 'cause and effect'. This translates into Williams' feelings of guilt, shame, and inferiority that take over in these scenarios. For a primitive mind, these secondary emotions are beside the point because they have nothing to do with what the individual needs to do to put the situation right. (We explore the fallibility of cause and effect further in Chapter 6—*A Quantum Prehistory*).

Clearly, ostracism is a commanding social tool that can have a lot of influence in social situations, regardless of whether we are primitive or modern. In civilized hands, it can become messy, but within the structure of a primitive tribe it is triumphant. For this reason, there are few reports of actual cases of primitive ostracism today because there is rarely cause for it to occur, proving it is an effective control. It is important to reiterate that it would not work without the 'reverse dominance hierarchy' structure, which places the majority of the tribe in power and the deviant at the bottom of the pile with nowhere to go but back to the group.

Where's the glory in modesty?

The promotion of non-primitive traits such as ambition, boastfulness, and pride, prevents the process of ostracism from protecting those natural principles for which it should be used. If we were to apply ancient tribal principles to modern people today, competitors at the London 2012 Olympic Games would be instantly ostracized. We would consider their boastful and conceited behaviour to be intolerable. The hot bloodedness we admire in our sportsmen and women is a potentially lethal quality in a young tribal man. Richard B. Lee's stunning ethnography of the !Kung Bushmen in the 1970s records the words of a tribal elder talking about a young hunter:

> 'When a young man kills much meat, he comes to think of himself as a chief or a big man and he thinks of the rest of us as his servants or inferiors. We can't accept this. We refuse one who boasts for someday his pride will kill somebody. So we speak of his meat as worthless. In this way we cool his heart and make him gentle.'

In contrast, a headline taken from the BBC website, official broadcasters of the Games, demonstrates a different set of social values:

> 'Greene's father praises arrogance—The father of Great Britain athletics captain Dai Greene says his son's arrogance has served him well as he starts his bid to win Olympic gold.' (3 August 2012)

Many Olympic sports such as marathon running, javelin, shooting, archery, and boxing have their roots in hostile and war-faring exploits. With this in mind, and considering the dire implications that Lee alludes to, what would sportspeople do with their self-confessed aggression and arrogance if we had not invested so much in an industry where they can express these qualities and not feel embarrassed or ashamed? From a tribal perspective, our world leaders would also be cast out, guilty and humiliated, due to their obvious desire to dominate. Hunter-gatherer nomads would quickly drive our high-profile politicians to the bottom of their reversed hierarchy. What they demand from a leader could not be more different. He (or occasionally she) must not show any signs of selfishness or personal aloofness. Generosity, impartiality, and gentleness are prized.

'Leaders do exist but their influence is subtle and indirect. They never order or make demands of others, and their accumulation of material goods is never more, and often much less, than the average accumulation of the other households in their camp.' *Richard B. Lee*

This is a flavour we find in many accounts of tribal life across the world: if there is a leader at all, he will put himself last and behave with modesty at all times. The tribe will select an individual for the role of chief based on their ability to demonstrate humility. Modesty and a lack of pride and self-importance are vital factors that ensure individuals in influential positions do not become intimidating or dangerous. The role of a leader must also be free from any accompanying power or favours so that jealousy does not develop within the tribe. No one should be inspired to fight them for their position. In primitive tribal life, no one should 'want' to be chief.

Some of the rites of passage and systems of ridicule employed by some tribes are also effective ways of eliminating arrogant and self-centred behaviour. By the time their young men reach adulthood, negative ego-oriented traits will be a rarity. The !Kung Bushmen tease and ridicule their young men so that they do not become big-headed. In this way, their elders encourage them to put the spirit of the tribe above their own personal needs. Bragging and boasting are associated with immaturity. Once a young man has successfully met with his adulthood initiations, such as making his first big kill in the hunt, these traits should disappear.

Primitive tribes are rarely found praising their young people as a way of encouraging good behaviour. Acting generously should not attract attention. It should be performed with modesty, and it is distasteful to expect praise for it. This quality is at the heart of primitive altruism. The initiations of a primitive young man at the onset of puberty often involve controlled deprivation and sometimes intense physical pain. This is so these juvenile traits are broken, and a mature, responsible, and dignified adult emerges. This kind of attitude to social relationships is one that does not breed expectation or envy but generosity and helpfulness. It is in harmony with the dynamic of the tribe.

In the West, we play it very differently. Through positive reinforcement and reward expectation (or what psychologists call *operant conditioning*), we encourage an individual to yearn for adulation and reward in return for doing something they should do selflessly, even anonymously, for the sake of the tribe. We seem to have entered the realms of a *Brave New World*,

whereby rewarding good behaviour rather than penalizing un-
desirable behaviour is the way modern society is controlling the
activities of its individuals.

> 'The nearly perfect control exercised by the government is
> achieved by systematic reinforcement of desirable behav-
> iour, by many kinds of nearly non-violent manipulation,
> both physical and psychological, and by genetic standardiza-
> tion.' *Aldous Huxley, Brave New World Revisited 1958*

Huxley's diagnosis of the future in his novel *Brave New
World* was formidable in its accuracy. We could be mistaken for
thinking this extract, taken from one of his essays twenty-seven
years after the novel was published, is referring to a modern
Western government. In fact, he is talking about the government in his novel which is set in a time hundreds of years from
now. As the author says himself, 'The prophecies made in 1931
are coming true much sooner than I thought they would.'

Operant conditioning is not a term that refers to the mind
control of a fictional and mesmerized future society, even
though it sounds like one. It is an accepted method of social
control in the twenty-first century. It is used and approved by
governments, school teachers, parents, employers, and behavioural psychologists. The widespread use of this behavioural direction shows us how far we have drifted from the primitive
idea of social responsibility. We no longer encourage our children to search for an intrinsic set of values. Even if we could
agree on what those values should be, external systems of reward now override the development of any innate drive to adhere to them. It seems that in the eighty years since Huxley
looked into the not-so-distant future, we have stopped teaching

our children to behave appropriately for the sake of what is appropriate. They are no longer rewarded with priceless values such as maturity, confidence, and self-respect, but instead by the sweets, the new toy or the excellent exam results. It is true that *operant conditioning* works, but when we approach behavioural control in this way, we are no longer breaking the destructive traits of the child. They are merely put aside as the controlling factor—the false incentive—diverts their attention. Individuals are then left to carry self-centred traits into adulthood. There they continue with their expectation of reward in a world that no longer consists of sticker charts and lollipops, but of gold medals, corporate bonuses, and knighthoods.

Tribal domestic harmony would be in peril if elders were to allow destructive traits in a young individual to prosper. As well, from a tribal point of view, enchanting an intelligent and emotional young person with superficial incentives and the constant promise of compensation is belittling. It also subdues any innate sense of responsibility that would otherwise develop. Stopping negative traits in their tracks in this way is not seen as cruel. In the modern world, we underestimate how psychologically nourishing acting responsibly towards one's group can be. It is long-lasting, unlike the sweets, toys, and pats on the back. It also ensures the individual has a place to belong. As we have established, even modern people want that. Our million-year-old man will look at the Olympic stadium in London and see a children's playground: a giant podium constructed of immaturity and boastfulness. It is the result of having lost our childhood initiations.

A fate worse than death

Whether we are a human being, an animal or an insect, ostracism in the wild can be a death sentence. When we lose our bodies at death, we become invisible to those we have loved and shared our lives with. If there is no spirit that endures or transcends—as atheists believe—death becomes a complete extinguishing, a finite and absolute end.

Primitive people believe that in the land of the dead or the ancestral realms it is certainly not lonely or isolated. When someone dies, every effort is made to ensure they pass smoothly over to those realms because no one wants to end up as a ghost stuck between worlds. However, even as a ghost you would be likely to meet up with other ghosts, so even that is favourable to the ostracized realm where there is no one at all. If you have behaved according to your tribe's laws throughout your life, then when it ends your ancestors will meet you and invite you to join them. Tribal life *and* death are sociable scenarios, so in primitive terms, the only place where loneliness reigns is within that ostracized space. A vital component of the design is that you are absolutely alone, with no one to care for you, support you, or even notice you. From a primitive point of view, it is truly a fate worse than death.

It is clear that ostracism plays an important role in the management of primitive life. The primitive dimension cannot accommodate rule-breakers and ostracism is an effective deterrent and punishment. Within the social make-up that supports this ancient process is a version of time and space that consists of qualities. Individuals' feelings and thoughts resonate openly and cannot be hidden. Our intentions—the drive behind all that we do and say—are on public display. They are intertwined with social rituals as part of a synergistic weave. Our resentment or arrogance, if we have any, then become part of that weave. Unacceptable as they are to the primitive code of conduct, nature must throw them out. In this dimension, there are no hidden realms within which we can escape detection. There are no cupboards where we store our desires and no laboratories where we transform our feelings. All thoughts and intentions are authentic and plain to see. There are no masks and no deviations. If we *feel* like we do not exist, then *we do not exist.* This world is extremely direct. This is the world of our ancient man.

A lonely existence

Many people today feel isolated. Entire countries are ostracized by the rest of the world on grounds of religion, war, politics or economics. In societies around the world, minority groups are shunned for a variety of reasons. In the West, we find retirees going back to work because the isolation of their retirement is unbearable. Individuals within their own families can find themselves neglected or misunderstood. Cases of depression, anxiety, and addiction are rife and increasing. Psychological problems such as these are often prevalent in people who are missing a sense of belonging or community in their lives. In modern times, it seems we are born into a world of exile because the element of exclusion has been woven into the foundation of what our world is made of. We have built an entire civilization in the penal colony. It is a place that should be ritualized, where we are not supposed to live permanently, and which is so excruciating that we should not be able to survive—yet here we all are. It is clear that not everyone is able to tolerate this scenario. It is having a significant impact on modern culture and our mental health as we try to adapt to accommodate life in a dimension where aloneness is a normal part of life. For many, modern society has become an unbearable environment to have to exist within. Only within a social framework that has exclusion as an intrinsic component can individuals live in such harrowing isolation when they have committed no crime, when they have done nothing wrong.

Adding to this, our idea of a community cannot cope with the vast numbers of individuals and the contrasting views, feelings, and desires they are entitled to express. While many people feel isolated in their communities, by the same token, nowhere else in the natural world are individuals allowed so much unprincipled free rein. As a species, we demonstrate a lack of cohesion that is beyond words. Out of this chaos, we strive to create new codes of conduct which will restore some sort of order, yet we cannot agree on the values that should make up such a framework. The natural foundation that we shared as primitive humans has become irrelevant. The intense focus on our physical bodies and the external environment perpetuates this situation. We are living in a penal colony. We are imprisoned by the belief that there is nothing more but the three dimensions that contain us. There is nothing beyond this most basic physical and linear existence.

'In the great dark between the stars there are clouds of gas and dust and organic matter. Dozens of different kinds of organic molecules have been found there by radio telescopes. The abundance of these molecules suggests that the stuff of life is everywhere.' *Carl Sagan, Cosmos*

When we look up at the stars and lament about life on other planets, why is it that we cannot find any? Most cosmologists agree, it is likely that there is life somewhere out there in some shape or form. But for now, the silence from space continues to ring in our ears. Perhaps we are not supposed to find it. Perhaps it has been arranged that we can't. Perhaps human society is a liability according to 'others' in the universe because it refuses to adhere to the principles of the primitive planet it occupies. Ostracized and abandoned, we must make our own way, alone. It is as if the rest of the cosmos is going about its business but with the door to Earth firmly shut. And we are outside in the cold trying to pick the lock.

CHAPTER 4

The Growth Gutter

'...human beings are no longer born; we are grown.'
Morpheus, The Matrix

A t the heart of our solar system is our daily guide. The sun not only rises and sets every day, but journeys away from Earth and back again throughout the year—or so it seems. The sun's daily voyage entwines with the seasons and the natural cycle of birth, growth, and death. Before we started to farm, we would only have had three seasons—spring, summer, and winter—to represent this cycle. Winter solstice in the Northern Hemisphere represents the sun's farthest point from Earth, and during this time in the mythical West, we experience a death. In the stillness of winter, amidst the darkness and the silence, everything natural grieves the loss of the largest and most generous entity in our world. The earth becomes cold and hard; no living thing has the heart to grow. The naked trees look petrified in the eerie midwinter light as if life will never overwhelm them again. Death in winter is absolute. Everything in the natural world enacts this dramatic finale, except human beings—who go shopping.

Progress and development, which in the West these days involve a lot of shopping, are at the centre of modern culture. A desire to grow and develop motivates us, not just in a physical sense, but also in our sense of achievement and self-esteem, and of course financially. We aspire to reach our goals and fulfil our ambitions. Throughout our lives, most of us strive to be the best that we can be. This is because our parents and society generally encourage us to approach life in this way. The most acceptable model for modern human social life is to pursue a constant betterment of one's situation.

The principle of growth also underpins our broader economic and political structures. Over time, systems must expand, develop, and improve. This approach to life has been in operation for thousands of years, since the Neolithic Revolution at least, and is modern man's most reliable template for success. But it has a downside. Structuring our lives on this linear model means that we never spend any time in a particular place. We never arrive at a destination and make a home there. As a species, we are always travelling from one thing to another. Constantly moving away from one thing and towards another furnishes us with an obsession with past and future. With this mindset, we have invented the concept of evolution, and we fit everything we find in the universe into this arrangement. Modern human nature is such that we must consistently outdo ourselves, work towards breaking records, continually refine and perfect what we do and the things we create. We develop as groups and individuals, our knowledge, culture, and economics, by expanding on our intellectual and material world. This is the modern human condition. The constant need to develop and change is what sets us light years apart from all other species in the natural world, including our ancient man.

Birth, growth . . . and growth

For the most obvious and reliable demonstration of growth, we must look to the natural world. There we find natural growth is a phenomenal, cyclical process. Primitive life in nature acts according to its instruction—it is another of the primitive laws. But, we cannot consider the natural principle of growth without also including the principles of birth and death. Together, they combine to create a life-process that is fundamental to our forbidden dimension. They are inextricable from each other. The line that says where one ends and the next one begins is indiscernible. It is like trying to work out where the colours of a rainbow begin and end.

We witness this natural cycle coming to life in the physical world year in, year out, within the changing seasons. The natural world spends the summer growing, bursting into a crescendo of activity. With the turn of the season, nature's slow out-breath begins, the sun moves away and the earth stops growing, the leaves turn and fall, and everything starts to die. Darkness takes over. It is cold and still. Nothing stirs. This is midwinter: the end of the out-breath where there is no breath at all. The earth has become barren, and there is no heat in the sun. The trees are but empty silhouettes against a grey sky of half-light. Then, nature starts her vast in-breath, and the light and warmth begin to return. We start to see signs of life and growth again in the celebration that is spring. Summer solstice is next, another moment of stillness as nature's breath stops, her lungs fit to burst with all that has led up to that moment. The extraordinary imagery of this cycle, which we witness over and over again, is the physical realization of nature's principles and qualities. This is nature's ritual.

Human physical life follows this arrangement too, just as animals, birds, and most biological organisms do. We stop growing at some point in our teenage years. We then start to mature until we meet middle age where we start our decline towards old age and finally death.

The sun's journey through the day is the most uncomplicated and symbolic example of the cyclical nature of growth. We experience it coming up every morning, travelling through the sky, and going down again every evening. The cycle never changes. The sun always behaves in the same way. From a primitive perspective, it is acting out one of the oldest rituals in our physical world.

In our science-led dimension, where matter is spiritless and dead, this performance is no longer a phenomenon. This is particularly so when we consider that from our perspective it is Earth that travels round the sun, and not the other way round. But, if we use a little imagination, we can wonder what might happen if the sun chose not to go down one evening. What if dying every night was becoming rather boring and he decided to stay up for a little while longer? Life on Earth would clearly be in trouble. Imagine a never-ending day, no dawn or dusk, no darkness or rest, just daylight all the time. It is a spine-chilling thought. Applying consciousness, in particular the ability to choose what to do with one's time, to a giant fiery ball of hot plasma and gas is ridiculous. But if we consider the sun to be a vast, ancient spirit with a powerful intention, as prehistoric people would have done, such a scenario becomes possible.

In a primitive world, where linear time is non-existent, the day can only be the day until night falls and it is no longer the day anymore. That is to say, we are only dealing with the experience of a day and not how long it lasts in terms of hours. We would be unaware of a passage littered with a series of events occurring one at a time and ending with night-time. Like a dream, we would experience what is happening as it happens and then something else that is happening as it happens, and it is all anchored in a ritualistic and symbolic framework. Now, if this sounds like the recipe for a huge headache, we must remind ourselves that in a primitive world, we find social order within these cycles, rituals, and behavioural laws. It does not lie within the structure of a linear sequence. Linearity in the way our minds have learned to perceive it is unnatural. It is a psychological framework that humans have developed that allows them to manipulate nature. But it comes with a variety of all sorts of problems that we are now struggling to manage. It is not necessarily the case that 'past, present, and future' create a stable framework for reality. If the thoughts and intentions contained in that past, present, and future are not adhering to natural laws, or even to the same laws, then humankind is in for some real bother.

The trident

Within the birth, growth, and death cycle we find a cardinal template for biological life on Earth. Our ancient man had direct access to this template. He observed the laws within it with rigour. We could say he was their guardian by the fact that he adhered to them without question. And so, he did not change. Guided by his elders he grew up, matured, and died and that journey did not take a number of years. Passage through space and time and the capacity to evolve only come into play when that cycle has broken.

An eternal cosmos that renews in cycles is not a new idea within philosophy and religion. There are variations, such as in the Hindu religion, where birth, growth, and death equal creation, preservation, and destruction. The universe is continually being born, growing up, and dying in a constant state of cyclical death and renewal. The main point of variation from a primitive perspective is the *integrity principle* and the unconscious awareness that accompanies it. To reflect with objectivity on the cosmos means we have already left the place where those principles live in their entirety, flawless and intact.

In the primitive dimension, where animism is the language of its occupants, the sun is an authority because 'he' sets a standard. He demonstrates through his daily and yearly rituals to every living thing, including our million-year-old man, how to exist—how to be born, how to grow, and how to die. In so doing, he provides the conditions for life on Earth. This establishes the sun as an authority, not just because he is powerful in

a physical sense, but because he demonstrates another fundamental primitive law: altruism. Primitive ancient people would
see great value in his gold light, a manifestation of the intention
that the sun shares with the world. The phenomenon of sun-
worship within tribes worldwide and throughout time is well
known. The sun is the most continually revered of all the spirits
or gods, and we will look at this in more detail later on in the
book. For now, we are talking about the sun's behaviour as a
ritual. It is his acts of benevolence that translate into greatness.
It is his unerring generosity that made him powerful in myths,
and that still inspires the natural world to grow during the summer and to grieve when he disappears in the winter—as a ritual.

If we are primitive, we have an obligation to return the favour; it is simply good manners. Reverence of such a god comes
in the form of reciprocation. This is the basis of millions of
years of human social life. Giving and sharing are at the heart
of every primitive community, and it begins each morning with
the light of the sun.

Ethnographic examples of this moral code in action are
plentiful. Acting out rituals of generosity and exchange are ancient practices that are still in operation amongst some primitive tribes today. Gift economies and ceremonial exchange
systems are still active in certain parts of the world such as Pa-
pua New Guinea. There, we find communities treating 'property' as a social relationship and not as a thing. We find the
potlatch (meaning 'give away') in parts of the American North-
west, Polynesia, and Melanesia. The ritual of sharing keeps the
moral code alive in the people who act it out. Community relationships and tribal alliances are at the heart of these ritualized

exchange systems. The principles of obligatory exchange and mutual aid differ from the more modern principles of trading because of one critical factor: the giver is the winner rather than the loser. Primitive exchange relies on giving, receiving, and reciprocating. It is the economic fabric of a primeval society.

In Western market economies, if we want something we make a demand first then we pay an agreed price and in return we get the thing we want. Scarcity, among other market influences, will determine what that price will be, but without the demand there is no market. I have a demand that you can fulfil so we make an exchange. In contrast, in primitive life, the act of giving stimulates the act of receiving something in return. Primitive people do not make demands: I will do what I need to do *first* then what I need will find me. This attitude again demonstrates a framework wherein dominance cannot take hold. If we have the givers as the winners, then self-interest is not a part of the process. This is an essential principle that keeps simple, primitive life working as it should.

The building of an economic structure from demand and expectation such as we have fits with our obsession with progress and development. It has also led to the upkeep of an absurd level of abundance. We have developed an appetite for 'stuff' that is not available in the natural world. It started with simple crop growing. During the Neolithic Revolution was when we started to develop a taste for demand and control with regard to food production and lifestyle. The Industrial Revolution was the pinnacle of those developments. The variety of products now available to us is simply ludicrous. From an environmental point of view, this level of superabundance puts the natural world under enormous pressure. It is a pressure that nature cannot endure indefinitely. In a primitive world, we accept gifts from other tribes who have access to natural resources that we do not, and vice versa, but we do not put an order in for things that do not exist. Without a demand as the prompt for an exchange, we can sustain an unchanging but flexible society, which is compatible with primitive relationships. In the modern world, the concept of money has taken over from relationship as our main currency. Like spoken words and the miles across France, we value hard cash in the place of our obligation to share whatever the natural world has to offer.

Another example of primitive socioeconomics turning modern principles upside down is the concept of competition. Without the element of competition in modern markets, the consumer—the one who is making the demand—is vulnerable to high prices and poor service. Fairness and cooperation are no longer values intrinsic to the exchanges we make. Therefore, we encourage competition in business and trade so that good customer service can return to the exchange via companies' sales and marketing strategies. Yet in tribal life, competitive behaviour will result in your exclusion. It is the very factor that will corrupt the values which the modern world employs it to uphold. As a self-serving concept, competition conflicts with any intention to cooperate and share. This is one of the many reasons why organizations that commit to corporate social responsibility, or that endeavour to put principle before profit, find it so hard to put into practice.

The role of hospitality in the Greek myths also illustrates the importance of generosity in ancient times. Zeus, the father of the gods on Mount Olympus and the most powerful deity in the Greek pantheon, is the god of the sky and thunder. He sits upon his throne surrounded by his four winged enforcers—Strength, Victory, Rivalry, and Force—who protect him and assist with his affairs. He is the bearer of the Aegis, a great symbol of authority and higher spiritual power. He is the keeper of oaths and despises liars. He is also the patron of hospitality. When mankind does not honour the principle of hospitality, Zeus sends his winged enforcers to intervene. From a modern point of view, it is a little curious to have an authority such as Zeus overseeing the provision of food and shelter to strangers, a social principle we do not consider important at all. But, he demonstrates to us that the principle of generosity was once sacred, and therefore worthy of his protection.

The obligation to share is another example of a significant principle that has diminished to something of little importance by modern civilized standards. But the ritual of fair exchange that we are discussing here is the Higgs boson of the ancient world, a golden rule that sustains the template of birth, growth, and death. Just as the Higgs particle gives weight to matter in a subatomic world, giving and sharing keeps human beings together in a primitive world where matter is not a factor. We could say that good manners make the primitive world go round. This may sound a little condescending, but only if we view politeness as the shallow etiquette that it is today, rather than a powerful precedent at the heart of society.

'The society with high synergy is the one where virtue pays.'
Abraham Maslow

Abraham Maslow in his book *The Farther Reaches of Human Nature* provides an example of this principle at work as he describes a 'giveaway' in a Northern Blackfoot Indian tribe. During a Sun Dance ceremony, the chief of the tribe lays out everything he has accumulated over the past year. He presents all his worldly goods to the rest of the tribe, consisting of piles of blankets and food, even crates of Pepsi. He struts about in a lordly manner, telling his people how hard he has worked and how he has managed to acquire all these things. Then, with 'a gesture of great pride, but without being humiliating', he gives it all away to the most vulnerable members of his community:

> 'At the end of the Sun Dance ceremony he was stripped of all his possessions, owning nothing but the clothes he stood in...in that process [he] had demonstrated what a wonderful man he was, how capable, how intelligent, how strong, how hard-working, how generous, and therefore how wealthy.'

For these North American tribes 'rich' is a reference to their values and not their material wealth. The qualities make them wealthy. The values they demonstrate are all the gold they need. The truth is that without them, their community and way of life would not survive.

In contrast to this native attitude was an item on the news recently covering the 2012 U.S. election. Barack Obama was pursuing a second term in office. His campaign focused on appealing to the less wealthy and promising higher tax rates for the top one per cent of earners. On the golf course, an investment banker responded with indignation: 'Get educated, get trained, and get a job'. Everyone has the opportunity to be as rich and successful as he is, so why should Obama penalize *him*?

In civilized society, individuals are no longer obligated to help those who are worse off than they are.

Please sir, can I have some more?

Nevertheless, we are aware of the worldwide economic problems currently facing modern life. The financial world is tumbling down the rabbit hole to a place where we have never been and know little about. We witness affluent Western countries dealing with diminishing standards of living and high levels of unemployment, poverty, and homelessness. This is due to austerity measures imposed by governments that are trying to reel in monstrous mountains of debt that have run out of control. The global economy is like a runaway train or a plane with engine failure. We are powerless to stop it.

Of course, the principle of constant growth is the foundation of economic policy in the West. Politicians and economists believe that economic growth is the way out of poverty and the way to avoid going into poverty. The financial health of Western economies relies on the constant expansion of the production and consumption dynamic.

But our economies cannot keep growing forever. Infinite expansion is an unviable concept, just as a sun that shines forever will not sustain life in the long-term. Richard Heinberg sums up this point amusingly in his book *The End of Growth*: 'Imagine...the survival challenges faced by a two-pound hummingbird.' Perhaps we would think it refreshing to have one long day and no night-time. It could be productive, we could go to the beach at midnight, summer would never end. But, as absurd as this scenario sounds, it is not so far from the truth. In economic terms, we have indeed created a constant summer and a perpetual harvest. We are stuck like ghosts in a groove that has worn deep.

> 'Notwithstanding the fact that bringing the Jerusalem of economic growth to England's green and pleasant land has so far conspicuously reduced both the greenness and the pleasantness, economic growth still remains the most respectable catchword in the political vocabulary.' *E J Mishan, The Costs of Economic Growth*

Many environmentalists are also scathing about economic growth because of its impact on the natural world. The fact is the planet cannot sustain the current rate of production and consumption. Add to that burden an expanding world population that has just doubled in the last forty-five years. A significant obstacle on the path to solving this problem is that our economies do not consider the natural resources in the environment as limited. Western governments treat natural resources as if they are infinite because they constantly renew themselves. In principle, this makes them limit*less*. But, the natural world is a system that runs in cycles and according to strict laws. It perpetuates itself via its own renewal based on the birth, growth, and death process and its occupants must not interfere with that process. We are interfering. Our constant consumption and the accompanying waste are in conflict with natural growth cycles. We have set up the illusion of a never-ending day that nature cannot sustain. The denial of this chronic state of affairs, such as we have seen in Western politics over the last half-century, is starting to look dangerously foolish.

It appears that if we abandon the ritualized processes that exist within nature, which, as the sun demonstrates, are the fundamental systems concerning life in our world, then we are going to meet with problems. One of those problems is that if we are acting out only a fragment of the cycle, we are not actually growing at all but stagnating. Although we are expanding, we are not maturing, and so unable to complete the cycle.

Herman Daly is an economist who studied environmental sustainability while at the World Bank for eight years. In his book *Beyond Growth: The Economics of Sustainable Development*, Daly talks about the ecological carrying capacity of the planet as a finite system. He believes that countries should move towards a system of 'steady-state' economics. This would entail a massive shift in accounting. Governments would account for natural resources supplied by the environment, not in terms of *income* gained from an infinite source, but as *capital* gained from a finite source. As well, two further issues would need addressing: the growing consumption of the developed world and the increasing population of the developing world.

Working with Daly's ideas could revolutionize the current situation. They would be a step towards slowing down the pace of change and allowing us to enjoy the view for a moment or two. Yet these ideas are so contentious that it is impossible to discuss them openly, let alone consider them as inspiration for any future policy changes. Politicians have never found the subject of population control a viable topic of conversation, and that is not likely to change any time soon. But this approach, this change in attitude, could form the basis for economic policy that upholds the primitive principle of *not changing*. A 'steady state' economy is one where we would relieve the natural world of our obsession with growth. We would also stabilize our levels of intake and waste production. So why are those who are in a position to affect economic policy so dispassionate about the state of our affairs when the problems we face are catastrophic? The accumulating debt of the West is now so large that we may have already reached the point of no return. Yet we continue to listen to politicians around the world having the same conversations about 'how to boost growth'.

> 'Money fetishism is alive and well in a world in which banks in wealthy countries make loans to poor countries and then, when the debtor countries cannot make the repayment, simply make new loans to enable the payment of interest on old loans, thereby avoiding taking a loss on a bad debt...The international debt impasse is a clear symptom of the basic disease of growthmania.' *Herman Daly*

Nature's laws state that there must be a death. Death is waiting in the wings because we cannot take the growth principle in isolation. If we work with this natural cycle, which we are obliged to because it is the source of our physical existence, we must have it in its entirety. Death must follow. If we do not instigate maturity and death ourselves, then nature, like a severe parent, will force them upon us. After all, we have to abide by her terms and conditions to some degree while we reside in her territory. The stronger and longer we resist this natural directive the harder it is going to be for future generations. The unavoidable consequences of keeping something alive when it is time for it to die are not going to be pleasant.

The current situation in the Eurozone is an apt example. Since the global recession hit in 2008, we have seen near-bankrupt economies in the Eurozone such as Cyprus, Greece, Portugal, and Spain bailed out by the European Central Bank. The crippling terms and conditions that accompany those loans create an unhealthy dynamic between the suffering economies and their 'bailors'. These ailing countries are bound to acts of self-interest by the robust economies such as Germany that do not make decisions based on the well-being of the 'bailees'. Instead, they act to manage the financial contagion solely to avoid infection themselves. It turns out that Europe is not the strong union of member states we might have imagined, but a group of inward-facing and self-serving individuals. Some are frail and on life-support as the terms of their bailouts slowly crush them. The cooperative relationships they needed to manage the legacy that constant growth has bequeathed have not materialized. The mythical void sits and waits with gaping jaws.

Comparing the global economy to the cycle of a fiery ball of gas or saying that our world leaders have an inherent fear of death may seem a little far out for most people. It is true that some of these ideas are hard to apply with conviction in the modern world. Primitive principles no longer work here. The foundation of modern living is so different to that of nature and the primitive world that these ideas end up sounding absurd. The primitive dimension is made of qualities, like our self-effacing axeman and the affectionate sunlight. The civilized dimension is composed of matter, of *stuff* that is mechanical and dead because we uphold the physical action over the quality of intention. Unfortunately for everyone involved, nature's principles are liable to come into effect at some point because nature and her laws are still responsible for the creation and support of biological life—for now.

Delaying the inevitable

We can track the trigger for constant growth, the establishment of demand-triggered economies, and the avoidance of death right back to the Neolithic Revolution. About 10,000 years ago we moved away from the nomadic hunter-gatherer lifestyle into one of farming and settlement. During that time, we started to lose the ability to find the things we needed, and we started to learn how to take charge of the things we wanted.

An important point to make here is that it is not the act of planting, harvesting or building a home in one place that is revolutionary or problematic. How we get our food and where we sleep is not particularly relevant in the scheme of things. Nature's laws do not dictate whether we should sleep in a hut or in a cave or in a barn. It is the desires and intentions that drive those changes that are incompatible with primitive laws. It is the control, demand, self-interest, and so forth that cause all the damage. These are the invisible influences that in modern times we disregard, but which are the potent driving forces of our world, then *and* now. As well, along with planting seeds came the firm grip of time. As we plant, wait (hope), and harvest, linearity transforms the cycle of birth, growth, and death. The focus is then no longer on the quality of the seasons, but on the expectation of what they will bring in the future.

With farming on this scale, we meet again with the trigger for thanatophobia (fear of death) in Western culture. The capacity to delay death as we grow non-stop has led to the development of many ethical and psychological problems relating to *not* dying.

In Western society, euthanasia and assisted suicide are moral issues of enormous contention as we question the quality of life of people with severe disability and chronic illness. Life expectancy in the West has never been higher. But when we discover that people who are over the age of sixty-five take up two thirds of our hospital beds, we must ask ourselves what sort of living this is. Are we living longer or are we just postponing death for as long as we can? In 2012 in the UK, we saw the case ruling of Tony Nicklinson. He battled with the High Court for his right to die after a catastrophic stroke in 2005 left him paralyzed with locked-in syndrome. He was unable to speak or move and claimed that his life was so unbearable and undignified that he was desperate to end it. He requested the aid of doctors to help him as he could not do it without assistance. The Court ruled against him.

So how does the introduction of farming lead to a discussion about euthanasia? What does controlling food production have to do with helping people to die? When we move from nomadic hunting and gathering to sedentary farming, communities experience a population expansion. We can feed more people on a regular basis. We start storing food, which is useful on the occasions when the crops fail. Our population grows, our life expectancy also grows, and so our relationship with death starts to change. It is this change in the way we relate to death that is significant and relevant. (In Chapter 7—*Death Materialized*—we discuss our modern attitude to death in more depth). Again, living longer, being well fed, and not wanting to die are not ideals that are in dispute. It is the principle of engineering and taking control of those natural processes that conflicts with the integrity of human social life. In a tribal situation, Tony Nicklinson would have died soon after his stroke. His family would have mourned the loss of him and then found the means to move on with help from the rest of their community.

Agriculture amounts to feeding more people and more babies being born. Hunter-gatherer societies in general have higher infant mortality rates than settled farming communities. Some primitive tribes believe that up to the age of six or seven a child might even choose to leave this life. For this reason, parents are more psychologically prepared for that event than civilized families are. This does not make it any easier when they do lose a child, but it means they have an inherent understanding and acceptance that young children do die. Primitive hunter-gatherers keep their population balanced using means that civilization does not always approve of, such as infanticide and senilicide. They also have low birth rates, which further lessen during times when food is scarce. Their population always reflects the carrying capacity of their environment. It is another fine example of their lack of demand. In the developed and developing worlds, our right to bear as many children as we want is a law unto itself. We do not relate it to nature, our environment or even our personal circumstances. We have the right to produce children even if we are infertile or if we do not have the means to feed and clothe them. If the planet does not have the resources to support them, the right still stands.

So, to conclude on this part of the story, we have identified two heavy-duty laws that belong to the primitive world. They are both crucial in our search for the forbidden dimension. First, the birth, growth, and death cycle, within which endings must occur so that something new can begin. Second, the principle of reciprocal exchange that forms a template for social and economic relations. What we have not identified are the factors that prescribe these laws. What are the invisible elements that compel unconscious, animal-like people to act them out without deviation? Whatever those factors are, they are forces that we moderns are unable to detect. Perhaps it is simply that we can no longer recognize them. Perhaps nature herself has removed them from our eyes and ears, as she waits, hopes, for a death to occur.

CHAPTER 5

Sacred Dimensions

'...we probably offend the spirits of things all the time, and because
we have not been polite they will be against us...'
Carl Gustav Jung

'Sacred' is a word that expresses a variety of devotional, spiritual, and religious sentiments. Here, I am using it in relation to the primitive act of sacrifice, an ancient practice that in most cases civilization disapproves of. This is the principal theme of this chapter. I am also referring to a 'sacred dimension' as something that is original and uncorrupted, a complete world operating in accordance with primitive laws. Thus, it is worthy of respect but not in a sensational way. Our ancient man will not think his reality is sacred because to him it is quite normal. What we would describe as divine or religious power is simply the life-giving, untiring vitality within nature that he is integral to. From a primitive perspective their 'world of spirits' does not equate to our mysterious ideas about religion. For people a million years ago, the sanctity of life would not involve *worship* but an unconscious and unerring *commitment* to a specific way of living.

Sacrilegious attitudes

The general picture we have today of prehistoric humans is not much improved from the Victorian portrayal of ignorant savages. This is one of our greatest obstacles to finding this invisible world we are searching for. Most of us still tend to interpret 'primitive' as 'substandard' which is more of a judgement than a true definition. ('Original', 'not derived', and 'of the beginning' are more accurate interpretations.) We think of ancient primitives as low-grade, ape-like humans residing in our past, and not as natural beings who live in a different dimension of perception and understanding to us.

An item on TV recently featured a mother of four complaining about the aggressive behaviour of parents at her children's football matches. She described their 'purple-faced rage' and 'Neanderthal behaviour' as 'horrific'. Referring to Neanderthals as savages in this way is commonplace. Yet we know that aggression of the kind she is referring to would be intolerable to the egalitarian make-up of Neanderthal society. They cared and shared, just like our axeman. So how has such an incorrect picture of the past, involving our primitive ancestors and their culture, come to be the acceptable version of events for us, their descendants? It is safe to say she would not have referred with such offence to any native person with whom we still share the planet. Still, the contemptuous attitudes toward indigenous people in more recent times are comparable to the way we continue to view those in our prehistoric past.

Another recent programme—Prehistoric Autopsy—featured Neanderthals in the first of three hour-long explorations into ancient human life. The programme presented us with three new theories as to why Neanderthals might have died out: climate change, cooperative breeding[1], and that they grew up too fast. They also suggested that Neanderthals were starting to develop culture and even art before they disappeared. This is a monumental claim in anthropological terms for which they presented no meaningful evidence. It is my view that we should be cautious when crediting items found at Neanderthal sites, such as shells or eagle claws, as evidence of art or adornment. Subjectivity taints our propensity to assign intelligence to primitive people who show signs of symbolic culture. In other words, when we interpret items from these sites as symbolic, we must be aware of our desire to paint the Neanderthal personality in a likeness that we can relate to, or in a way that we find engaging. As well, it is quite wrong to insinuate that the expression of art is an antidote to savagery when there are so many peaceful tribes around the world who do not adorn themselves at all. When we widen the picture and consider the primitive psychology we are studying, it is difficult to argue against the traditional theory that Neanderthals died out because they did *not* develop culture. Their primitive psychology would have been immune to progress and so could not have crossed those boundaries.

This tendency to distort the facts crops up a lot in archaeology and anthropology and any study of past events involving

---

[1] A hideous term that refers to a social hierarchy of 'breeders' and 'helpers'.

humans. It is sometimes uncomfortable for us to look the past square in the face and acknowledge the atrocities, as well as the achievements, that our species has accomplished. We must be careful that this discomfort does not prejudice our interpretation of what we find in the ground.

On the other hand, I do not intend to romanticize or idealize a primitive lifestyle in any way. I aim to present another perspective by looking at the primitive psychology and comparing it to our own. My intention is to question some of the conventional ideas about the primitive mind and its perception of life. I believe that many of the current problems we face as a species are due to the way we perceive the environment with complex civilized minds and not simple primitive ones.

Falling apart at the seams

We know that global systems are under huge pressure and re-introducing primitive principles could be a way of relieving that pressure. But would the average person be able to apply any of these values considering their incompatibility with the way we live now? We would have to change at a fundamental level to embrace anything that primitive life has to offer, even if we did think any of it made sense. We would need to view events in our lives through different eyes. Deep-seated psychological connections that our minds have fused together over the last few thousand years would need defusing. This may be too much to ask considering our low opinion of the terrain we are exploring. And then there are our genes. How do we reverse the genetic evolution that has accompanied us through the phenomenal changes in thinking and lifestyle? In an ideal world, we would take bits and pieces from the primitive model that we can adapt to serve our civilized way of life and leave the rest as there is far too much to lose. Now we have created it, we cannot live without it. But if we continue to see nature as a platform constructed from biological organisms, geological formations, and weather systems, with no intent or spirit and no power over mankind's destiny, will any primitive principles we adopt have any effect? How can we work with nature and create a new and sustainable world if we are unable to communicate with the 'thing' that provides us with a world in the first place? Our senses no longer register the signs, symbols, warnings, and guidance from nature and the primitive otherworld. It is this animistic guidance that directed our axeman through his life thousands of years ago and stopped him from changing. As we cut the cord of our primitive life support, we introduced a new code of conduct. We embraced a different attitude towards our responsibilities as a species of planet Earth, one that would change the face of human life and the planet forever.

Most people who agree that civilization has gone too far still want the future of society to look something like what we have now, even if they acknowledge that we must make substantial changes. But if we cannot go back to the primitive, where do we go? What model do we use that is viable for our children and that of the natural world we are destroying? The place to which we are travelling does not seem to be on any map. We do not know where it is or how to find it. It is as if we are afloat on a large sea and there is deep water stretching away to every horizon with no land in sight. Mankind has been afloat like this since the Neolithic Revolution. A long, long time has passed in which we have forgotten what it is we are looking for. Each day we wake and consciousness washes away any lingering ancient memories or dreams. We look out across the desolate, watery expanse and think, 'Today we'll find land'. But we don't. We can't. The natural laws state that we can only pass through to another life if we know first how to experience death. To travel through the figurative doorway that leads to a renewed existence, we must know sacrifice: the ability to give up or let die that which is important to us.

The curse of sacrifice

Despite its religious nuance, sacrifice is a straightforward law in primitive life. We must lose, or give up, something of value so that we know humility. If we do not then we will know deprivation, and probably resentment too. To make a sacrifice is to offer something of value *to* something else. It may be to give thanks or to bring good luck and fortune to the tribe. It is also a primitive loophole ritual to deprivation: surrendering a little of what we need ensures that we know how it feels to live without it.

Let us take the winter solstice period as an example. Christianity aside, Western traditions have treated midwinter as a time of sacrifice even in more modern times. This time of year has also been a celebration of the sun in many cultures in the Northern Hemisphere. The ritualistic generosity of the sun nourishes the earth, keeps us warm, and encourages life to flourish. So as the days grow cold and dark through wintertime, ancient people would pray for the sun to return. As part of that prayer they might give something up in exchange for their request. As we discussed in the previous chapter, in a primitive world we cannot make a demand without first making a contribution—it is against the law. The act of sacrifice then binds them to the values of the sun and the cycle of life it represents.

Christianity has 'borrowed' this ancient ritual from nature and relocated it to springtime. Jesus dying at Easter has a similar significance, as the custom of Lent demonstrates. If we feel inspired to make a sacrifice or to give something up according to Jesus' principles, we are bound to him and the values of Christianity instead. Ramadan in the Islamic calendar demonstrates a similar notion of imposing abstinence to show religious devotion. The original concept of sacrifice that exists within these religions came from the loss of the sun—an event that we continue to experience every year. There are many religious festivals today whose roots are also found in the ritual honouring of sacred light as a deity: the Chinese lantern festival, Hanukkah, the Jewish festival of lights, and Diwali, the Hindu equivalent. On a more pagan note, historians tell us that Vikings sacrificed boars to the goddess Freya, or they rolled giant wheels of fire down a hill. All these rituals were once in honour of the sun as it disappears and leaves the world destitute and dying. They are humble demonstrations by people whose lives depend on this natural entity returning, so that life can begin again.

In ancient times, the sun was an icon that represented certain qualities and values. The monotheistic gods of our modern religions are also representatives of principles and values that their followers commit to. Therefore, taking part in the festival or the ritual binds the devotees to those values. As atheists or non-theists, we imagine that we are not taking part in this exchange. But, when it comes to the natural world, *everyone* is taking part, it is just a question of what in. The rituals and festivals within these religions were in their origins acknowledging an event in nature that affects us. So as atheists, are we excluded from these effects, or are we just ignoring them? If we remove the deities and their values altogether, whether it is God, Allah, or the Sun, we are free to turn a traditional ritual of sacrifice into anything we like. Should the solstice period become a ritual involving expectation, indulgence, and extravagance, it makes sense that we will be bound to those principles instead. This seam at midwinter is significant. It creates the enchanting atmosphere that we in the Christianized Northern Hemisphere now associate with Christmas. As modern society sits upon nature's platform, this seam must apply to us in all its glory, whether we believe in it or not. While we are able to deny the existence of God or Jesus due to a lack of observable evidence, we cannot deny the darkness that has engulfed our lives, and the sun—the basic fuel for complex life on Earth—that has diminished.

The primeval ritual fight between light and dark is one of the oldest in nature. We find it in the myths and stories of most cultures. Many of us can relate to such a battle in our lives and within ourselves. It is present as a moral fight between good and evil within most religions, and it is the basis for many poems, stories, and films. If we continue to witness the original, ritualized battle every year between the Sun and the Darkness, what does it mean for modern human beings who no longer take any notice? What effect, if any, is it having on our lives while we are busy shopping and wrapping gifts? Before we can answer these questions we need to look at the ancient perception of 'seams', as they play an important role in primitive life and are relevant to this part of the story.

A seam in primitive terms is the join between one place and another. Examples include the horizon, a riverbank, dawn, dusk, waking from sleep, and falling to sleep. In traditional cultures, spirits in the otherworld use seams to travel through to the physical world, and as mere mortals we would be mindful during the moments they occur. They are times or places in which influences might enchant us and whisk us off to other dimensions; or spirits or ancestors might give us a message or a warning. When a seam is present, all sorts of positive and negative influences can take hold. Therefore, seams are the circumstances, or ingredients, that allow portals between worlds to appear. The traditional death and rebirth of the sun at winter solstice is an impressive example.

People in traditional cultures believe doorways hold a powerful magic. They are gateways of transformation that can influence us and our environment. The ancient Greeks painted a sticky tar around their doorways to stop unwanted spirits or influences from entering the house. In the company of traditional Mongolians, it is polite never to step *on* a threshold when one enters a ger; we must always step *over* it. Many primitives consider that a doorway has the ability to record us. As we pass through it, we stamp the door with what we are, as if it takes a photo of what we are thinking and how we are feeling at that moment. That imprint could then linger and affect those who go in and out of the door afterwards. The magical properties of a door lie in its ability to take us from one environment to another—to transform. Whether it is from room to room in a house, from inside to outside or from day to night, this transformation needs to be clean; in other words, without influence.

The symbolic time at winter solstice is a significant seam through which influences can pass, whether we are aware of it or not. It is the same as stepping over a threshold into something or somewhere new. Unlike us, ancient people would have been watchful of these influences while they went about their business. If they were careless or absent-minded, they could find themselves somewhere they did not intend. Even today, we can walk from one room to another only to find that when we arrive we have forgotten what we went there to do. What influence was in the doorway that we passed through that made us forget? Whose thoughts were lingering there from earlier that we unknowingly collected on our way in?

We shall never surrender

From a primitive perspective, the loss of ritual sacrifice and the clean process of transformation have contributed to some of the social problems we have today. Are we benefitting from acting out ceremonies around the values of expectation and consumption at Christmas, instead of sacrifice and letting go? According to primitive psychology, we should not disregard the influence of the sun's ritual as though it bore no relevance to us. Nature is providing us with a 'signal to act'. Our carer, landlady, and teacher is sending us messages that we should be interpreting and acting upon. But we ignore them and choose to go shopping instead.

The commercialism we have developed at this time of year is in conflict with this natural cue to let go. Incessant human consumption is not only devastating for the environment, but it is also a principle that is incompatible with nature's primitive laws. Self-indulgence, greed, and vanity are all reasons for your tribe to ostracize you. As we have discussed, gifts are integral to primitive survival because they serve an economic system based on the social values of giving and sharing. They are not superfluous knick-knacks that will go to landfill in a few months' time.

There is a traditional Romani custom where the clan gathers round the campfire at the winter solstice. Everyone asks the fire to take away the things they want to give up for the new year. It is similar to our tradition of new years' resolutions. The spirit of the fire, *Yag,* takes the unwanted items to the spirit of the sun, *Kam,* where they will perish. As he dies his midwinter death, they will die with him. Hindus call this practice a *Yagya* or *Yagna,* whereby the fire (in Sanskrit also *Yag*) purifies our spirit, home, and family. Many traditional cultures associate fire with ritual sacrifice and the sacred qualities of the sun.

Joining in with this natural ritual at this time of year ensures we are binding ourselves to values that are simple, compatible with nature, and carry no loopholes. If we do not, we may find ourselves fixed in a twelve-month contract with whatever principles we were demonstrating during that time. Thanks to the natural power of this seam, those are then bound to us for the rest of the year. This process will continue every year, until we decide to sacrifice them, something that will get harder with each year that goes by. In the end, we stop noticing the binding and the pressure it brings with it. Those factors that are within the bind—expectation, disappointment, greed, self-pity—have grown with us and are now a part of what we are. We have transformed, but in the wrong way. Once 'letting go' becomes 'taking away', the transition from primitive to civilized is complete. Liberation turns to emptiness.

Ancient human beings must have blended with this midwinter ritual but not in a ceremonial or deeply spiritual way. Any profundity would be in the instinct with which it is acted out, just as it is for the autumn leaves as they fall from the trees. As a dualistic kick against the physical world, spirituality has no place in an integral, animistic world.

The primitive laws demand that sacrifice is a reciprocal exercise. When the tribe next door gives gifts of food or animal skins, we return the favour. When the sun dies and the earth makes room for new life, again we do the same. Only then can we experience new life within the coming year. In tribal life, there is always an exchange. In Christianity, this sentiment is also apparent. Jesus dies in springtime and inspires Christians to make their own sacrifices in return. His death ritual prompts Christians to be humble and more mindful of God and his principles. The difference between the original ritual and the Christian copy is the moral sword that Christianity wields. Giving up what we do not need, whether physical or psychological, is not prompted by the threat of guilt and damnation in a primitive world. It is simply practical and respectful to the natural laws that govern our species.

There are many primitive rituals across a variety of cultures that honour the sun and attempt to encourage him back to chase away the shadows of the dark and the cold. There are also many stories and myths about the art of sacrifice. One of the most pertinent to this story is that of the Minotaur.

Holy cow!

In Bronze Age Minoan Crete, King Minos ruled from his throne at the palace of Knossos. The ancient people of the island of Crete were surrounded by the sea and so bound by the powers of the god Poseidon. They believed that his influence protected them from invaders. The Minoans were professional seamen and socially quite sophisticated. They worshipped an array of gods that related to the natural elements. But the Minoans' reliance on the spirit of the sea meant they were rather slow in their development of the warrior class that was running amok throughout the rest of Europe at this time. Their faith in Poseidon's power to protect them was steadfast and as a consequence their culture was untouched for thousands of years. Poseidon was revered. Many offerings and sacrifices were made to him in return for his divine care.

The legend of the Minotaur sits outside any chronology and tells of a day when Poseidon brings Minos a great gift: a sacred white bull. This creature had strength and beauty that Minos had never seen before. Its magnificence mesmerized him. Accompanying this gift was a condition: Minos must sacrifice the bull in Poseidon's honour. Of course, he agreed. But when the day came for him to fulfil his oath, Minos could not go through with it. The beauty of this sacred creature had such a hold over the king that he did something unthinkable. He betrayed Poseidon, the wonderful spirit who had protected his kingdom and his people for so long. He placed the sacred bull within his royal herd and sacrificed another bull in its place. It was inevitable that the great sea god would notice the deceit and he blew up in a rage. His revenge was swift and came in the form of a curse on Minos's wife by Aphrodite, the goddess of love. She enchanted Pasiphae, an immortal daughter of the sun-god Helios, to fall in love with the sacrificial bull. Pasiphae's passion for the beast was unrelenting. She instructed the carpenter Daedalus to build a wooden cow covered with cowhide in which she could stow away. Concealed within the royal herd she made love to the sacred creature. She was soon found to be pregnant and bore the Minotaur, a monster with the body of a strong man, but whose head resembled that of its father. Pasiphae nursed the monster and it grew up fast. In no time it was terrorizing the island, killing and feeding off the innocent people of Crete. Even in the face of such horror, King Minos and Pasiphae could not bear to kill the creature. Instead, they built a labyrinth, an impossible maze where they hid the monster deep inside the dark and confusing tunnels. It would never get out. Every nine years, the beast would feed on nine young people from Athens. On one of these occasions, the Athenian hero Theseus, driven to save his people from slaughter, went into the labyrinth and killed the beast in its lair.

Many who comment on this extraordinary story focus on Pasiphae, her adultery, and the debauchery of mating with a bull and creating a hybrid monster. But from our primitive perspective, we will focus not so much on the sexual act but on the sacredness of the object. In this myth, the sacrificial object lives on. Minos does not surrender it in the traditional ritualistic way. The result of a moment of such weakness and indulgence is the birth of a monster. Therein, the ritual becomes a reality. The story warns us that if we do not honour a sacred process in ritual, it becomes a tale of horror in the everyday lives of those who betrayed it. The ritual is covering a loophole (see Chapter 2).

The tale of the Minotaur is poignant in this story about primitive life for a number of reasons. First, if we miss the cue from nature for straightforward, ritual sacrifice (such as at winter solstice), we must meet with the inevitable results. And every time we do, it will become more difficult. If we miss our prompt, the loop is set in motion again and it becomes harder to put it right when it comes back round. As a mother, Pasiphae cannot bear to kill the monster, so they find a way to accommodate it.

Second, Pasiphae acts out the idea of taking something too far. She should reckon with her desire for something that is sacred and forbidden, but she does not. She ritualizes the insatiable hunger for something magnificent that is out of reach, unprincipled or bad for us. She also enacts the devastating consequences should we give in. Through the story, we can learn the lessons without having to act them out ourselves.

Third, while we are busy casting judgement upon Pasiphae, we forget that the real culprit is King Minos. The love affair with the bull began with him, and innocent Pasiphae reaped the consequences. This point is of great relevance. In primitive cultures, young men need initiation rituals to stop their egos from developing. Initiation in primitive life is a simple ritual that promotes humility. Sacrifice is also a ritual that promotes humility, so sacrifice must be part of the initiation. We find it in the challenges where we need to let go, so we can move on to new experiences without dragging the past along with us. It is a simple but vital principle.

We could go so far as to say that this myth tells the story of the last 10,000 years. The practice of sacrifice in human social life no longer exists. We do not enact it as part of a prayer. We do not even engage in the modern psychological unloading of disagreeable intentions. But the monstrous consequence of that missing ritual now occupies not a labyrinth, but our new-found inner worlds. There, we honour it with sinister sacrifices and offerings of our own, just like the Minotaur. We feed it every time we are too weak to say no to our children or when we turn a blind eye to deception between friends, when we eat too much, or buy those shoes we do not need and cannot afford. Within these seemingly insignificant moments, we are feeding something dangerous within ourselves, which we quickly dismiss with a shrug. These moments arise from the intentions and emotions that are driving them: complacency, lethargy, self-pity, vanity, negligence, and disdain. These are absent in a primitive world because they are non-intentions and non-emotions. These non-things give birth to the apathetic monster I am describing. If we allow such a creation free rein within our inner worlds and we lose the power to control it, we will have set up an identity too introverted and self-serving to ever undo. Our personal minotaurs will have us as slaves.

And now, there is no hero to save us. There is no one who possesses the sunny, sacrificial qualities such as Theseus had.

The heroes we adulate now are Olympians. Athletes uplift us and bring us together. They inspire us to focus, work hard, and exercise. Except they are not ambassadors of humility rushing to rescue us from our anxiety or fatigue. So the monster lives on, buried inside our personal labyrinths of consciousness, unquestioned and unbroken. Egoism, greed, expectation, and demand are now legitimate human sentiments. We have rebranded them as self-worth and necessity, hope and prayer. These traits will grow every year at the winter solstice when we renew our contract with them, courtesy of the natural world.

Legends in the making

In the Hindu religion, we still witness the reverence of the sacred cow. In parts of India today, cows wander the streets and shops. They peruse people's gardens and potter about the roads stopping traffic. They are free to roam wherever they please. No one interferes with them due to their sacred nature. Within the Hindu faith, cows symbolize strength and selflessness. Although they are no longer sacrificed, they are still a symbol of what that once expressed.

Now let us cut to the Western world where cows have long since lost their sacred identity. In 2008, the British government granted a licence to Newcastle University in the UK which allowed them to produce cow-human hybrid embryos. The argument in favour of this controversial research is that it is a process that can supply science with stem cells for research into untreatable diseases. (Scientists use cow eggs instead of human eggs because human eggs would be unethical and so donors are in short supply). The embryos that the researchers created were

99.9 per cent human and 0.1 per cent cow. The ethical debaters erupted. The pro-life campaigners, Roman Catholics, and other religious groups were up in arms. As they protested, they asked questions about human rights, human dignity, and the sanctity of life. But from the perspective of our primitive story, our invisible ancient man wants to ask: what about the dignity of the cow? Coming from a human who lived unchanged for a million years, we should not dismiss this question as merely childish or ignorant. We know that just a few hundred years ago, cattle were sacred not only in India but across much of Asia and Europe. So we could rephrase the question: what are the consequences of leaving the animal's spirit out of the ethical debate?

Today, it is illegal for a person to engage in a sexual manner with a cow, even though we are unable to conceive an actual Minotaur. The biological laws pertaining to humans and cattle cross-breeding make it impossible. But it is not illegal to use cow eggs and human cells to create hybrid embryos. Therefore, we are creating a potential life that resembles the Minotaur on the premise of creating a supply of stem cells. Scientists are bringing a myth to life as the point of this extraordinary story collapses into our physical dimension via a laboratory in Newcastle. The metaphorical Minotaur is solidifying. A simple story of sacrifice and its message has no meaning now because we dismiss it as *just a story*. But if we do not heed the warning that the ritual provides, it becomes 'real' life. That is its power. That is the curse of nature that we disregard.

These terms and conditions, or rules of engagement, are nature's way of keeping her primeval universe in order. Ancient stories and myths are remnants of an age when our intentions were out in the open and dealt with. From this point of view, it is a risky business to dismiss nature as a submissive backdrop that we think we can manipulate and control forever.

We witness the consequences of removing the principle of sacrifice from human life most acutely in the natural world. Every species of animal, bird, and tree is left wanting in order that a minority of humans can experience a life of superabundance without ever knowing modesty. Natural crude oil took 300 million years for the Earth to create, but it will disappear within my lifetime because civilized culture does not value moderation as a social principle. Loggers are clearing the Brazilian Amazon rainforest at a rate of approximately 6,000 square kilometres per year. This operation threatens the wildlife and indigenous tribes who live there and contributes to the rising temperatures of the planet. There is no way that the Earth will ever replenish these lost treasures. But what will we do when the natural world runs out of these riches? What will our personal minotaurs do when we no longer have pointless objects with which to feed them? Will we ever be able to give up the things we do not need for the sake of our future, or for the sake of the Earth itself?

At the end of 2013, we are experiencing a global economic recession, plus food and energy crises. Each year roughly 925 million people in the world go hungry, 7.6 million people die from cancer, and 1.8 million people die of AIDS. Never before has the human race been so vulnerable to so many critical factors affecting its future that it cannot control:

'We are seeing a perfect storm of converging crises that together represent a watershed moment in the history of our
species.' *Richard Heinberg, A Primitivist Critique of Civilization*

Yet the advancement of technology is phenomenal. Technological development during these turbulent times is head-
spinningly fast. It is a field of clarity and endeavour that shines
like a lone star on a dark night. It provides humanity with a
legitimate means to express its insatiable drive to progress.
How does the development of technology fit with the cycle of
growth in nature? How will the natural world accommodate
the rapidity of this development, when everything else is falling
apart at the seams?

CHAPTER 6

A Quantum Prehistory

'The Moon! Artemis! The great goddess of the splendid past of men!
Are you going to tell me she is a dead lump?'
D H Lawrence

We have so far established that the primitive dimension within which our ancient man lives is one consisting of qualities and intentions and is invisible to our eyes. Quantum physics describes a nano-dimension that is also invisible to our eyes. It provides a mathematical description of the behaviour of energy and matter at a nanoscopic level. It describes a hidden reality that reflects the primitive dimension in many ways as it abides by similar principles and laws. As individuals who live in the macroscopic realm, we are unable to see or access this subatomic world, but that does not mean it does not exist. Science tells us it exists, so we believe it to be true. The way we question the existence of God, a magical otherworld or a realm teeming with spirits, but not the existence of a quantum universe illustrates how rooted our physical mindset has become. It is also an example of the extent to which we trust scientists. However, if science were to have an otherworld, quantum physics would describe it.

The principles at work within a quantum system are not consistent with the physical laws of our more familiar three-dimensional world. To start with, these principles only apply in the miniscule dimension that is home to atomic and subatomic particles such as neutrons, electrons, protons, photons, and quarks—the tiniest reduction of matter that there is. For some reason, when matter gets this small it starts to behave in a way that is at odds with the normal-sized things we can see.

For instance, in the physical world we can make accurate predictions about the behaviour of things, but in the quantum world we can only predict a more vague probability of a pattern of possible outcomes. Physicists call this a *probability wave*. A simple example is that of throwing a ball. If we know certain information about the ball, such as its weight, position, angle, and speed, we can predict its trajectory with remarkable precision, and thus know where it is going to land. If we fired an electron in a similar way to the ball, the result would be a pattern of probabilities regarding where the electron might end up, as opposed to a conclusive, absolute position. This is because in a quantum system a particle does not exist 'somewhere', just as in the primitive world there is no geographical place. The particle exists in a number of possible locations and allocating it a specific position is meaningless. Within that system 'position' is an indefinable term. We could say the particle is nowhere as much as it is somewhere. 'Somewhere' is subjective and such subjectiveness we cannot apply to an electron, only to ourselves.

The human skew

Our ancient man did not live somewhere. Archaeologists may have found his million-year-old remains in a specific location, but his existence has far more in common with a quantum system because it consists of patterns and relationships within an entire system. The geographical place which his bones or tools occupy belongs to our idea of what reality is and not his. His meagre remains travel into our geography, like a fragmented image from a dream might travel into our consciousness in the middle of the day. But no matter how hard we try, it is a dream we cannot remember. The location of an object in this way is only possible in the world of classical physics where geographical definition within three-dimensional space is a concept we all agree upon. Our belief in three dimensions is so strong that we do not question it when we get up each morning and go about our business. Yet, our experience of this physicality is only *a perception.* And it is a perception that is actually quite new. It has evolved over time as our minds have adapted to accept that *this is how things are.* The environment, society, and the people around us train our minds with this version of reality from the moment we are born. There is no going against it. Some will argue that the collective perception of a population on a scale of this size is enough to equal an objective reality. I would argue that it remains an illusion if the population in question can only see part of the picture, nothing more than fragments of a dream. On the other hand, our million-year-old-man had the whole picture, thanks to the *integrity principle.* He was in the dream, and he never left it.

Adding to this problem—or maybe at the heart of it—modern humans do not experience first-hand much of what they believe to be true about the world. Science reports and we accept. Think of the moon. Our immediate encounter with the moon is as an ever-changing image of silvery light in the sky. It is an image we share with every person in the world, primitive or not, who is able to see. Many tribal people go further and attach a spirit to it, and often qualities too, which they also witness and interact with. In traditional Romani, the moon is the female *Shon*: illusive, watery and emotional, and sister (and lover) to the sun spirit *Kam*. In Norse, the moon is male, *Mani*, but also sibling to his divine sister *Sol*. In modern society, we believe that the moon is a big rock, a cheerless and barren quarry orbiting planet Earth. This is a perspective endorsed by the pictures of Neil Armstrong and company who landed there in 1969. To primitive people this description and these pictures, or indeed any other pictures, would be unacceptable evidence of the moon they know. It is not their experience of the moon; it is Neil Armstrong's experience of the moon. Even if we could take our ancient man into space from our dimension, or show him the moon through a powerful telescope, he would be unable to associate what he finds with the magical light in the night sky that he and his tribe may sing to or dance beneath.

In this way, the primitive mind only considers first-hand experience as real and something it can share with other primitive minds. This rule also includes night-time dreams. We know that the boundary or seam between wake and sleep is slight for primitive people. They witness dreams 'in person' so they consider them to be legitimate life experiences. This rule of first-hand experience ensures everyone agrees on everything. There are no debates about the moon, Earth or anything else. Everyone shares the same experience and that makes it a solid fact. This rule makes the primitive world seem small and intimate, yet it is a vital factor that ensures geography cannot get into their psychology. Out of sight, out of mind, is literally the case here. The moment we allow the concept of geography into the realm of perception we feel as if the world is expanding. But in reality, *experience is thinning,* like cosmic pastry rolling out across the universe, growing weaker and flimsier as it stretches. A substantial first-hand relationship with what we see and interact with is replaced by a limitless, but second-hand, *knowledge,* which we now accept as more real. An intimate world with no geography—or miles that we must travel—would be one where we are free to visit the moon whenever we wish, no space rocket required.

The modern inability to relate to our surroundings is an issue we have met before. The screen capture we looked at in Chapter 2 is an illustration of the way we have turned away from our environment in favour of a life on the inside. The image showed a screenshot of the document I was writing that I had dropped into the document itself to illustrate the modern process of internalizing experience. If we focus on that image alone, a mere snapshot of a moment in time, is it possible to achieve a true sense of what is going on when the original version of experience is happening in another dimension of perception altogether? A place where someone is in a room typing a document, which is an epic story in its own right. Yet all we have is a single, random page. This would be the scenario if you showed Neil Armstrong's moon to our ancient man.

Werner Heisenberg's *uncertainty principle* describes this problem of fixing a definition. Heisenberg was a significant contributor to the creation of quantum mechanics and won the Nobel Prize in Physics in 1932 for his work. His principle states that we cannot measure the position *and* momentum of a quantum particle at the same time. If we give it a defined position, then we freeze it in time like our screenshot. We exclude any consideration that it is in a state of motion or that it is interacting with other factors which may be influencing the state it is in. To define a position is to create a still image that interrupts the flow of the story. We will never know how it begins or how it ends. Life is not an event that we can look upon at a particular moment in time and expect to understand exactly what is going on.

This is also the case with archaeology. The ancient remains archaeologists unearth of our axeman provide a snapshot of a scenario. This snapshot does not reveal relationships or connections with the rest of *his* scenario, only ones that relate to *our* world and *our* perception of reality. We make assumptions based on our perception and experience of life as it is now. Just like the screenshot picture, we do not have in our hands anything like the full story.

The mystery of Stonehenge in southern England is an example of the uncertainty and confusion our subjective universe can cause. Stonehenge is a Neolithic monument whose construction bewilders historians and archaeologists. Situated on Salisbury Plain in Wiltshire, it mesmerizes people from all over the world who come and marvel at its sheer impossibility. According to the modern version of reality's structure—the 3D universal agreement of weight, geography, distance, and so on—Stonehenge should not exist. In the same way, the pyramids at Giza and many other megalithic monuments around the world should not exist either. The ability to manage the colossal weight of the stones and the precision engineering used to arrange them could not have belonged to primitive people whose technology and intellects were inferior to ours. But obviously it did. This suggests there was something at work that we have not thought of, something we will talk more about in the following chapters. For now, we will use Stonehenge as an example of how our subjective interpretation of prehistoric events hinders the exposition of the truth. We drag the stones and the primitive minds of those who arranged them into our dimension of time and space, just like the bones and tools of our million-year-old man. Here, we subject them to the classical laws of physics, laws that did not exist when Stonehenge began its life.

The popular theory at the moment as to what Stonehenge was for is that it was a shrine to the dead. Archaeologists believe people brought funeral urns in a procession from what they call 'the land of the living'—a prehistoric settlement about a mile down the road at Durrington Walls—to Stonehenge. There they honoured the dead in a mysterious ritual of ancestor worship. Experts portray solemn ceremonies among the stones. They paint a picture of Neolithic people journeying from all over Europe so that they may transfer their deceased loved ones safely to the afterlife.

We do not need to go into all the archaeological detail to appreciate that this account is, to a large extent, speculative. It supposes that Neolithic people, as well as farming, were developing spirituality and were thus inspired to build this extraordinary temple. This in turn would suggest that before the monument's construction, these people did not have a concept of an afterlife. But this theory does not fit with what we know about primitive thinking and behaviour. Extant tribes (and Neolithic people were still tribal) show us that primitive minds are remarkably easy-going about death and burial. In normal circumstances, they do not need extreme cult rituals, and certainly not on this scale, to relieve them of a religious need to bridge the gap between 'here' and 'there'. That need resides within our modern, dualistic psychology. This is the crux of the point I am making: the way we perceive the world today inevitably influences the way we interpret prehistoric behaviour. It is my view that there was a catalyst for the extreme behaviour at Stonehenge that most archaeologists do not discuss. We will explore this in depth in Chapters 9 and 10.

In the meantime, we also need to consider the political dynamic that had sprung up here along with the stones. We know of an elite and wealthy family—or families—interred in the burial mounds surrounding Stonehenge. They dominated the political scene. These individuals—kings and queens, sorcerers and warriors—exerted immeasurable influence on the people who lived in the region and any visitors and traders who were passing through. They controlled trade, settlement, agriculture, slavery, and the distribution of wealth. They also managed religion, and particularly access to the afterlife. This scenario was not one where the majority ruled, such as we find in egalitarian tribal life. Stonehenge was a seat of immense political and religious power. It mirrored other ancient monuments of its time around the world in this regard—the ziggurats in the Middle East and the pyramids of Egypt. Our familiarity with this kind of political hierarchy depreciates the massive impact its introduction would have had 5,000 years ago. Neolithic people would never before have seen such dominance and inequality in their politics and society. We can only begin to imagine what it was like to experience.

Another issue that exposes our desire for an agreeable account of history rather than an objective truth is the issue of human sacrifice. Considering sacrifice is often associated with monumental architecture in other parts of the world, we cannot rule it out here. Indeed, there are cremated remains at the site that look suspiciously like sacrificial remains in that they are all male and aged between 25 and 40 years old when they died. We should at least consider that those in command at Stonehenge may have been indulging in human sacrifice, whether we like the idea or not. They would certainly have had a motive. Controlling tribal people on this scale would have to involve tactics of psychological and social intimidation, of which human sacrifice could have been an effective component. From this perspective, Stonehenge is looking less like the local community church we know and love and more like a propaganda machine.

There are many ongoing debates about what happened at Stonehenge. There are also other archaeological examples that illustrate the dangers of viewing events significant to our social evolution from a vantage point of convenience. To consider the past only from where we stand now makes it impossible to view it without prejudice. Much to the frustration of quantum physicists, the hidden nature of the quantum universe also presents this point loud and clear.

The language of things

Returning, then, to the invisible quantum realm, another factor we need to consider regarding this problematic placing of a particle lies with the definition of it as a thing. We in our thingified world have thingified psychologies, so we cannot help seeing subatomic particles as defined things as well. In reality, their form is far less distinct. Within a minute quantum state, we are dealing with relationships and connections within a unified whole. It is the patterns that are relevant and informative: repeating patterns, interference patterns, of frequencies, energy levels, and waves. This way of describing and interpreting *a world* is reminiscent of an animistic and symbolic language, which also entails interpreting patterns and relationships within a unified whole.

Spoken language using words is a tool that we have developed to express our thoughts and feelings. But when we use words that are also things, our thoughts and feelings become things too. The complex language we speak today involves words that are objects, items that we place, arrange, and throw, just as we throw a ball. Words also have a linear sequential structure.

The definitive rules that govern this structure are such that the words we use to express ourselves in turn affect the way we construct our thoughts in the first place. *Linguistic determinism* is the term psychologists use to refer to the conditioning effect of language on the way we think. The same conditioning process applies to the language of mathematics. The nature of its architecture influences the way we view and interpret the world that it is describing. These languages are tools that we use to express what we think and feel. But the process is a two-way street. What we think of as a passive system is actually affecting what we choose to express, and how. This exchange illustrates how the simple laws of relationship and interdependency that exist within animism are at work even within a linear construct like language. It also tells us that we do not notice these principles at work in the background of our lives. So, as a rule, the inability to detect something is not grounds for claiming that it is not happening.

When experts discuss whether Neanderthals could speak, they look at their physical ability to construct the words, rather than their ability to convey meaning using sound. We can imagine that for the primitive Neanderthal mind, language would not have involved a string of objects in a line. For modern minds, words precede meaning. Understanding has become second in line to the explanation or expression itself. As a result, our messages have become less specific, not more, as we tend to think. This is not the case for animals and birds, and probably Neanderthals too, who use sounds instead of objects to communicate.

The call of a seagull is not a thing that has a place. It is part of a pattern of expression that connects the seagull to all the other seagulls in the world. If we take two seagulls two hundred miles apart, the seagull who is calling somewhere on the English coastline is the same as the seagull who is calling somewhere on the Welsh coastline. The seagulls and their calls are one and the same. If the seagulls are identical, where are they in terms of geography? How do we find their calls on a map? We could say they are a single object or a single being that can be in many places at once, similar to an electron. The theory of quantum *entanglement* reflects this idea. If we separate two quantum systems that are indiscernible from one another, we will still observe correlating behaviour between the two systems. Einstein described this strange phenomenon as 'spooky action at a distance'.

Every seagull has the properties of a seagull that make him a seagull and indistinct from all other seagulls. We could capture one, tag and track him. This would tie him to a defined place at a specific time and prove that he is an individual in his own right. But the place we are tying him to can only belong to our perception of reality. The seagull does not become aware of geography, time or individuality because we are tracking him. Instead, he remains oblivious as the *integrity principle* makes him immune to the concept of three spatial dimensions that we are trying to attach him to. He would carry on as an unconscious seagull in a primitive world regardless, albeit one wearing a tag.

This idea applies to everything in primitive nature, including our ancient man. He too would have had a call, perhaps similar to the Native American tribes, Maoris, or Australian Aborigines. All primitive tribal people use simple, pure sounds to express alarm, delight, excitement, and so on. These calls involve a consideration of the environment within which they live. A seagull's call will involve the air space, sea, cliffs, and clouds or rain, as well as the other seagulls around him. It is not a subjective expression from an isolated inner world floating about on its own, with no relationship to anything or anyone else. Nor does it have a connection to past or future. Birds, animals, and primitive people can only express what is happening at the time. This is a crucial factor in making sure they do not develop and change. It stops them from developing individuality. And it is the key concept that connects the physical natural world to quantum systems. Everything relates to everything. Each component must behave according to those relationships and not according to its own demands, desires, and beliefs.

The Pirahãs in the Brazilian Amazon jungle are a wonderful example of how this collective cohesion works within a primitive lifestyle. They apply a social rule called the *immediacy of experience principle* (Everett 2009). This is a rule that demonstrates the law of first-hand experience that we talked about at the beginning of this chapter: '...the Pirahãs only make statements that are anchored to the moment when they are speaking, rather than to any other point in time' (Everett). We could say the Pirahãs are immune to the arrow of time and its ability to affect the way we relate to our surroundings. The *immediacy of experience principle* excludes any influence past or future might have on them. For this reason, they are not able to refer to anything that is not happening now:

'...the Pirahãs don't store food, they don't plan more than one day at a time, they don't talk about the distant future or

the distant past—they seem to focus on now, on their immediate experience.' *Daniel Everett, Don't Sleep There Are Snakes*

In a situation where someone in the tribe has died, no one
will talk about them in a nostalgic way. Family and friends will
not reminisce about what they had experienced together in the
past, or what they might miss sharing together in the future. It
does not mean that they forget them, only that they do not
speak of them. The only time a Pirahã might mention an event
from the past is in the form of a story. They would tell it as a
social myth of sorts, but there always needs to be an eyewitness
to the original event present to ensure the *immediacy of experience principle* is upheld. Although the Pirahãs do use words, they
can substitute those words with a hum or a whistle without de-
grading their meaning at all. Theirs is a rare and constructive
way of communicating, which promotes their extraordinary
capacity to avoid change.

In a similar vein, the Romani Gypsy language has a word
collico. This word refers to both yesterday and tomorrow. For
traditional Romani people past and future are the same. They
wrap themselves around us like the air, rather than stretching
infinitely behind and before us. Likewise, the word *merriben* refers to both life and death, as both experiences are interchange-
able. According to tradition, the spirit of Collico is dangerous
but alluring. If you are not careful, she will mesmerize you. Her
charms are distracting. She will amuse herself with you, like a
cat with a bewildered mouse. Should you entertain her, she will
intoxicate you in such a way that you will not notice the damage
she has caused. In other words, she will curse you. The result of
this curse might see you becoming fixed upon a memory from

the past. It begins to haunt you and influence your behaviour in the present. Also related to the word *collico* is *locollico*. This word refers to a group of malevolent diseased spirits (the Locollico) and it shows the contempt nomadic people have for linear time. We can find references to the devastation that the concept of time can cause human psychology in many traditional stories and myths.

Many worlds

As well as the *uncertainty principle*—that which cannot position a thing in a place—the dimensional quality of the *integrity principle* is synonymous with another theory of quantum mechanics: quantum measurement. The difficulties physicists face with regard to quantum measurement relate once again to the subjective nature of our world of three dimensions. For a pure quantum state to remain pure, we must isolate it from the classical laws of our environment. Any interaction with these laws will cause it to collapse or spill over into it. Physicists call this collapse quantum *decoherence*. It is irreversible. It means that we cannot measure a quantum state if the measuring equipment (which includes us as observers) is located in our everyday world. The simple act of measuring will ruin the system. This theory also applies to the primitive world of our ancient man, and Neolithic Stonehenge to some degree. The influence of our subjective physical laws on scenarios that exist outside of those laws prevents us from seeing them as they are. So, how reliable are we as observers of a state, primitive or quantum, of which we cannot be a part?

Instead of the defined position of a particle, the *probability wave* we mentioned at the beginning of the chapter describes multiple possibilities of a particle's state or position. These multiple possibilities set the scene for quantum *superposition*. This is a theory which describes the ability of a particle to be in more than one position at once, rather like the seagulls[2]. Only when we measure or observe one of these possibilities from a remote and fixed position will it collapse into a single reality.

One way round this inability to observe more than one possibility at a time is to make the observer integral to all the scenarios as well. This way, we are not standing outside looking in but duplicated and set within the pattern of probability itself. Now we have many positions for many versions of ourselves to be in at once. They are all oblivious—or unconscious—of one another's existence. This is the basis of the quantum *many-worlds theory* and is a difficult concept for our linear and subjective minds to handle: my sense of self does not want to consider identical versions of myself in other realities doing all sorts of things that the real me knows nothing about.

We can look at this again in terms of animals and birds. Starlings, like seagulls, are identical. They all share the same qualities and attributes in that it is difficult to discern one from another. This is also the case for quantum particles, and probably for humans who were living on Earth a million years ago.

As the sun sets, thousands of starlings dart and dance together around the twilight sky like a shape-shifting apparition from the otherworld. As a single entity, they create sweeping

---

[2] Quantum *entanglement* is also a form of quantum *superposition*.

patterns that we could never predict due to the chaotic nature of their choreography. They are unable to learn the moves of their aerial dance beforehand. As we try to detect the principle with which they are determining the spontaneous moves of their ritual, their collective behaviour appears erratic. There are millions of possible patterns that they could enact, but only as one of those starlings would we understand how each manoeuvre and position is revealed to them. And, as the birds do not observe themselves, the dance does not collapse into a single defined reality—that only happens from our point of view. We could see the birds representing a *wave function*. Quantum particles (also indiscernible from one another) interact with each other and the forces at work in their environment. They create a variety of possible scenarios that we are unable to define because they do not adhere to laws that we can relate to.

To be in more than one place at a time is to blend with your environment, so you are the same as the next person in your species or your family. In order to achieve this, you cannot have a strong sense of self. You must be self-less. In this way, both starling and ancient man exist as part of a whole. The interdependence within that wholeness is where they will find their purpose and individuality. Their personal validity is not tucked away somewhere inside themselves but demonstrated in their interaction with everything around them—just like a quantum particle.

The *many-worlds theory* of quantum mechanics illustrates how different dimensions we moderns cannot perceive are actually able to exist. We are also starting to realize that our ancient man has more in common with a quantum state than he does with modern civilized society and psychology. We only view these quantum dimensions as many worlds from our limited perception of just one world, one *collapsed* world. If we were not living in a single measured reality, perhaps we would be able to recognize and experience all these dimensions. As our ancient man did not live in a state of collapse but within the unified whole, we can imagine that he had access to other dimensions, realities, and states as a matter of course. Perhaps he regularly travelled to the stars. Perhaps they, in turn, visited him. Perhaps the stars only seem far away because they exist in a world that we can no longer perceive.

Quantum ug

Quantum computing is the next step in our technological revolution. We are living in the Technological Age, so the achievement of quantum computing must be the pinnacle of that age. In theory, a quantum computer utilizes the principle of the quantum *superposition*, whereby we can have a variety of nonlinear states occurring simultaneously. In simple terms, a quantum computer works by replacing the usual binary *bits* 1 and 0 with quantum *qubits*, which are quantum objects such as spinning particles. The *superposition* capabilities of the *qubits* enable the quantum computer to make several calculations at once, instead of one at a time as with a conventional computer. In so doing, it can vastly reduce the time it takes to perform complex tasks. Professor Brian Greene, author of *The Hidden Reality: Parallel Universes and the Deep Laws of the Cosmos*, gives us an idea of the phenomenal speeds a quantum computer is capable of:

'...a quantum computer no bigger than a laptop has the potential to perform the equivalent of all human thought since the dawn of our species in a tiny fraction of a second.'

If, or rather when, we reach that link in the chain of discovery and scientists develop this technology, it will transform our lives. The information processing at virtually limitless speeds will catapult computer science down new science-fictional avenues. We will experience what it is to be part of a revolutionary period of human development, just as our ancestors experienced in the Neolithic Age. It is one that will change our lives forever. These developmental revolutions are awesome when studied in retrospect, but when caught in the eye of the storm as we are with this one, the permanence of what we are creating can leave us feeling a little uncomfortable.

One of the many major advancements that quantum computing will make possible is the artificial simulation of a convincing environment that can accommodate conscious beings. We know that scientists are able to recreate biological life using a computer. In 2010, a team of U.S. scientists presented us with Synthia, a viable synthesized genome of bacterium. The team at the J. Craig Venter Institute successfully synthesized the genome of the bacterium *Mycoplasma mycoides* from a computer record, and transplanted it into the existing cell of a *Mycoplasma capricolum* bacterium that had had its DNA removed. (During my research I noticed that many of the press reports refer to Synthia as 'her' and 'she', a sad irony when we consider how the sun and the moon are now known as 'it'.) So, as synthetic biology advances and Synthia becomes a plant, an animal, and then a human, all we will need is a suitable environment in which to house 'it'.

There are philosophers who think this might have already happened. It is not only in science fiction that we find ideas and theories about simulated realities, but in philosophy too. Perhaps our descendants in the future have developed this technology and we are the guinea pigs who are acting it out. We could be living in a computer simulation right now. We could even be sophisticated human versions of a Synthia-type synthesization. Considering the artificiality of the civilization construct and the disparities between it and our alleged primitive origins, these philosophical ideas are not difficult to contemplate.

In the cult film The Matrix (1999), we find a version of the computer simulation theory. According to the movie-makers, artificial intelligence (AI) has taken over the world. Human beings exist only as biological batteries providing energy to the ruthless machines, hence the simulated reality: to ensure humans are ignorant of their true existence. While this is a worthy plot for a film, it is missing a realistic motive that fits with our primitive story concerning primeval nature and cyclical time. Nature works in cycles, in which case we might assume that mankind is also travelling in a loop and will meet up at some point with circumstances and scenarios that it has known before. Primitive cycles ensure we revisit circumstances we have previously experienced. So while we are busy travelling the illusory passage of time, we are in actual fact going round in a cycle—nature's laws dictate this. Therefore, we are unable to elude certain experiences, even if we think we can. History *will* repeat itself. This means that the initiator of a simulation will reside somewhere back in our deeper past, even though he or she may also exist in our so-called future. (In Chapter 11—*The Paradoxical Machine*—I talk about how this paradox is likely to affect the future of human-machine relationships.)

If we have determined that the quantum dimension of nanotechnology is comparable to the primitive dimension of our million-year-old man, let us go further and suggest that the principles which underlie quantum computing are also familiar to him. If we take a conventional computer and imagine removing the physical elements, the hardware—wires, components, casing, transistors etc.—the invisible properties of what it can do in principle will be all that remain. These include the ability to communicate at near light speed, translate, store, and process information, record and replicate data, process complex calculations, and so on. Computers achieve all of this without travelling the linear 'bits in between', making each process immensely fast.

You might agree, I have just described a device that sounds like the human brain. The human brain is a phenomenal piece of equipment. One factor in particular is its ability to unconsciously multi-task. For instance, it can control your breathing, heart rate, and blood pressure, while you are driving a car and discussing the meaning of life with a friend. Now, imagine that the brain is not a physical thing either but an indeterminate quantum object integral to its environment, like the electron and the starling. Only once it has been measured or observed (in other words, become conscious) does it become the brain as we perceive it today—the curious grey object inside our heads. Half a million years ago, there was no brain, no consciousness, and no inside or outside. We would perceive the lightness of our form not unlike images in a dream, two-dimensional and weightless, similar to a digital image on our computer or television screens. Ethereal bodies like this would know little of gravity or time and space, and so would move like lightning from one point to another through the power of intent alone. There would be no travelling, waiting, or killing time. The 'brain' is the 'mind' with the capacity for what it can do in principle, but without the restrictions of existing physically or having to express anything physiologically.

It is plausible that the principles of quantum computing were available a million years ago if we accept that modern mechanistic laws did not apply then. This is particularly so when we consider that 'a million years' refers to another dimension of perception and reality, rather than a span of actual time. The *integrity principle* applies the theory of *superposition*, thereby negating the threat of collapse. Where we *would* see a collapse of the primitive dimension is if the social or ritual, rather than the physical, laws are broken. If our ancient man violated the clean, psychological fabric of his dimension with a dubious objective or selfish intent, then life would change. It would be irreversible.

The Neolithic Revolution was a period when humans considerably violated these primitive laws. The natural spirits and our primitive instincts began to recede, like stars in an expanding universe. Nature triggered the irreversible consequences of quantum *decoherence* and threw mankind into a purely physical world. Breaking the rules of your species means nature will isolate you, ostracize you, like a child is sent to their room. The unconscious connection you had with your environment will be removed. Three dimensions will thereafter form the walls of your prison, and Time will be your sentence.

This theory—that ancient bones and tools are piercing through to our perception of reality from another—explains in part why there are so few archaeological finds before the Neolithic period. The erratic human ecology and evolutionary discrepancies of the finds in general may not simply be because they are random remains that have survived decomposition. If we think of prehistory in these dimensional non-physical terms, we put whole periods of time into new contexts. Pre-Neolithic archaeological finds could be the result of specific moments of collapse that pierce this dimension from the primitive, original one. Someone puts their axe down with a misplaced intention, and it disappears. It is then dug up a nanosecond later by conscious people in the penal colony, who attach time to it because that is all *they* understand.

When we look at Stonehenge, and certainly the Egyptian pyramids, it is not hard to believe that prehistoric man experienced a vastly different universe to us, one that included access to a sophisticated, dimensional technology. Through the discipline of science we are discovering technologies that in principle have existed for millennia, but the invention of time concealed them from us. Now we can begin to explore what that means. What was it they were using to build these structures, and, of course, why?

Perhaps asking anyone to imagine a million-year-old mind as a computer might be asking too much, particularly considering such a mind has no capacity for cognitive reasoning. Jumping from the 'ug factor' to quantum technology is a considerable leap, to say the least. A quantum leap perhaps.

* * * * *

A principal function of this book is to reveal the technological capabilities of ancient primitive life. It is also to show how these abilities link to the natural integrity and animistic perception of a primitive mind. Could it be that there are forces within nature independent of the human mind that link these two worlds together? Science may be unable to identify this connection due to the restrictions imposed by consciousness and linearity. For now, quantum principles are a means of illustrating how a primitive psychology connects to modern technology and that modern *society* is something else altogether, something of an anomaly. How have we managed to lose the innate understanding that our ancient man had about the way the universe works? How have we managed to convince ourselves that presiding over rather than being integral to nature is a means for success? What went on in the deeper past that inspired mankind to create such an uncomfortable and unsustainable society?

Chapter 7

Death Materialized

'I'm not afraid of death; I just don't want to be there when it happens.'
Woody Allen

W e are laying the foundations of a theory: our familiar reality of three dimensions is a measured and collapsed version of a timeless and immaterial world. Today, we are living in a penal colony born out of the irreversible violation of Earth's primitive principles. One of those principles—the birth, growth, and death cycle—has been engineered at some point in the past in such a way that we find ourselves in modern times stuck in the groove of growth. We have lost the ability to move naturally through the cycle into death, and so into birth again. Modern people have developed an obsession with *not* dying.

A natural death follows maturity. In nature, winter follows the ripe summer, which we witness in the flaming colours of the falling autumn leaves and in the liquid gold light of a dying sun on a winter's day. How have modern humans developed such fear of an event that the natural world manages so elegantly? We go to great lengths to manipulate the process, by delaying it or even trying to avoid it altogether. Death is no longer a fact of life. It is not beautiful but archaic and unfashionable. Death is definitely in decline.

In Chapter 4 we touched upon some of the problems we have developed by becoming stuck in the rut of constant growth: overpopulation, people living longer and with pain and suffering, people even staying alive in bodies that are not fit for life. In this chapter, we will look in more detail at our bleak relationship with death. We will investigate how we have lost our ability to appreciate and celebrate death in a primitive way, and how many of us are now deeply troubled about what happens when we die.

A perfect world

In modern times, science has become the medium with which we can play with life and death. We can create life, recreate it, simulate it, and destroy it. The timeworn subject of human mortality no longer resides in the realms of myth, philosophy or theology. It is in hard science. The unveiling of a posthuman existence is in the hands of molecular nanotechnology and computational neuroscience, in the forms of cloning, digitizing, and brain emulation or uploading. Mind-boggling methods such as these, which interfere with human construction at a fundamental level, can affect us before we are even born. The genetic modification of an embryo has been possible for a long time, although the creation of designer babies raises many ethical questions. According to genetic biologists, modifying a human embryo's genetic material can eliminate a predisposition to certain diseases (for example, Mitochondrial disease) that a mother might pass to a child. With one process, whereby surgeons combine In Vitro Fertilization (better known as test tube babies) with cell surgery, there is a third person involved who donates an embryo that is unimpaired. One healthy embryo is then engineered from the two and inserted into the womb of the woman with the faulty genes.

From an ethical perspective, how acceptable is it to interfere with life at this fundamental level? How will this genetically flawless person feel when they grow up and find there is a third person in the biological parent mix? What parental rights, if any, does that third person have to the child? These are a few of the questions at the heart of this issue, and they are not easy to answer. Embryonic stem cell research, eugenics, cloning, and genetic engineering are all examples of mankind's robust desire to control the natural process of procreation. It is not only religious groups who find meddling with life at this rudimentary level disconcerting, but it is difficult to argue against it. The hard sell of curing disease has become impossible to dispute in a society as disease-ridden as ours.

These questions for debate are light years away from a primitive perspective. How would our million-year-old quantum axeman view this problem of ethics? Questions he is likely to ask are: why are you (again) focusing on the physical problems and not on the values and principles which that person is going to grow up demonstrating? What is the point of having a flawless genetic make-up if your spirit (or mind) is sick? In other words, how will you ensure that this perfect embryo is not going to end up as a bully, a free-rider, a social upstart, or even a murderer or paedophile? How can you be certain that they will grow up honouring the natural cycles of transformation, making a positive contribution to the community, and continuing with the unchanged principles passed down from their ancestors? These values must always come first. Without them, our ancient man's entire social structure would break down.

There are roughly seven billion humans on Earth right now, and that number increases by about 1.5 million every week. Yet those who are living *without* poverty, mental illness or disease, are a diminishing minority. We know the conditions for human life are worsening. The Western world is starting to experience some acute social and political problems that are not going to miraculously disappear. These problems, stemming from religious and political instability, financial corruption, government and personal debt crises, and economic austerity measures, demonstrate a crumbling fabric. Civilization is like a giant glacier that is breaking up and the cracks are growing bigger with each day. We can expect that over the next few decades civilized society will experience some uncomfortable impositions. These will be primarily in the form of food and energy crises and environmental disasters. At this moment, nearly half the globe lives in poverty with one in every seven people in the world going hungry on a daily basis. Yet we throw away *half* of the four billion tonnes of food that we produce each year. Environmental primitivist Richard Heinberg points out in his *Primitive Critique of Civilization*:

'We in the industrial world have gradually accustomed ourselves to a way of life that appears to be leading toward a
universal biological holocaust.'

From a primitive point of view, if we are living in these
dreadful conditions then we must have been excluded from
normal life. Poverty, depression, and disease cannot exist
within the original tribal template. These are the conditions of
people who have been ostracized; they are therefore destined
for an early death. The penal colony is clearly alive and well.

As we have already talked about, primitive social life is direct. It is based on sharing and respect for one another and the
natural environment. If people consistently show signs of deviance within that framework, they will continue to be ostracized. Ostracism, like death, requires a transformation to get
through it. It involves moving through a challenging experience. Our tribe requires us to transform in order that we may
return to them. If ostracism does not work (which is unusual),
if we do not change and we persist in terrorizing the tribe with
our bad behaviour, we might find ourselves being quietly dis-
posed of.

Suffice to say that primitive, egalitarian society is not based
on non-violence, as some modern pacifists suggest. The *choice*
of non-violence suggests a capacity for morality that is unknown to primitive people. The ability to decide to do the
'right' thing is not psychologically available to them. They are
unable to consciously analyze a situation in the context of good
and bad. Instead, ritual dictates their behaviour. The power of
the majority enforces values and principles that the tribe in-

stinctively share. The compassion we witness might be the result of egalitarianism from our perspective, but it is not the inspiration for it, as is the case with modern pacifism. In a
primitive world, altruism is not driven by unconditional love,
or by an innate moral sense, but by ritualistic and natural law.

Homicide is rare in tribal life. But if ostracism fails, it can be
an effective last resort. No sentimentality is present within the
tribal people who practise this form of social control, yet they
are affectionate, caring, and humorous. It is simply the case that
tribal life cannot tolerate disruptive behaviour. And as we have
already discussed, the reasons for that behaviour are not up for
debate. The primitive constitution states that our intentions
must always have the tribe at heart. Social values must be upheld at all costs. Those who love and protect you when you
honour those values will be the same people who will throw
you out and even take your life should your behaviour warrant
it. This is the primitive deal. This is what nature dictates, and it
is how primitive tribal life prevents disease from developing.
The shadows that bring disease are not, under any circumstances, tolerated.

So how do primitive tribes decide to 'dispose' of you if they
are unable to analyze the facts as we do in a court of law? In the
situation of your constant deviance, primitive people are no
longer able to see 'you'. If you are exhibiting vile or unacceptable behaviour 'you' are no longer present. The shadow that now
exists in your body has devoured 'you' and is masquerading as
'you'. Far from tribes taking it upon themselves to judge and
execute members of their clan in cold blood, it is more the case
that the individual in question has disappeared, and something

sinister has replaced them. If we look beyond the body, we start to notice that the spirit of the person we loved and respected is no longer present. When this happens, we must take action and remove the villainous influence for the sake of the group. They would see compassion in this context as entertaining shadows, and, therefore, dangerous. If a tribe tolerates this form of assault and if they do not protest in a direct way, these shadows will invite their unscrupulous friends to come and join them. This is a transformation that tribal people cannot allow under any circumstances. Otherwise, they will be overrun by negative influences, individuality will flourish, and the tribe will collapse. Shadows sweep quickly through a community if no one stops them, and with them they bring all sorts of social disruption, including disease.

Ritual healing

The Nyae Nyae !Kung Bushmen in southern Africa do not fear death. What they do fear are the spirits of thinness, hunger, and sickness: the bringers of death. The Bushmen live lives of scarcity rather than abundance. The shadowy influences that threaten them bring sickness in the form of deadly fevers, and bad luck in the form of a lack of food and water. Their Ritual Healing Dance is a remarkable demonstration of their collective force as a tribe against the death-bringers. Through their dance, they confront the dark influences who skulk about in the shadows waiting to fire their poisonous arrows at unsuspecting victims.

The whole tribe takes part in the Ritual. The men encircle the women and children, stamping and dancing in rhythm to their clapping and singing. The healers work themselves into a trance-like state. They dance like this for hours. They shout abuse at the spirits, threatening them and ordering them to leave their people alone. This is another example of a ritual that has developed out of social trauma, like the Ghost Dance we talked about in Chapter 2. It is a demonstration of the measures tribal people will introduce when modern problems such as sickness start to interfere with their lives. Indeed, the Bushmen were not sickly people, '...they were in good health, and their attention was certainly not morbidly concentrated on sickness. They were all thin but strong, wiry, energetic, and lively, much given to talk and laughter' (Marshall 1999). And the Bushmen are not alone. There are many examples of communal events where tribal people evoke and interact with the spirits—the Amazonian Pirahãs, the Indian Nayaka, and others. These events are not always solely for the purpose of healing. They strengthen the community while they engage in an animistic exchange with the otherworld.

The Bushmen and other primitive tribes like them have a significant problem to contend with as they strive to maintain their original lifestyle. While they are essentially primitive beings similar to our ancient man—instinctive and integral to their environment—unlike him they are caught up in our collapsed reality. They have to suffer the overlap between a timeless and immaterial dimension and a solidified penal colony. 'Unconscious awareness' (primitive) and 'conscious unawareness' (civilized)—two incompatible states of perception—have somehow been woven together. This clash of states imposes difficulties on tribal life. There are many examples of the conflict that can arise from such a weave.

One quite devastating example is that of colonization. This is the dimensional weave in its most loathsome form. From the Neolithic Revolution when 'pioneer farmers simply swamped the hunter-gatherers like the rising sea levels' (Miles 2005), to Columbus in 1492 when he met with the 'affectionate' Arawak Indians, civilization has displaced and extinguished indigenous peoples across the world. And it continues today: logging in the Amazon jungle, zinc mining in Mexico, copper mining in Myanmar, oil and gas exploration in India, tourism in Indonesia. All over the world, the principles of civilized society are destroying indigenous communities that had remained unchanged for millennia.

During the European colonization of the Americas, the settlers brought with them an invisible malice that was far more dangerous than they were: infectious disease. Small pox killed more natives in North and South America during that time than anything else: 'Their population had been reduced in the four hundred years of recorded history by as much as 95%,' due to a 'viral and bacterial innocence' (Page 2003). In a monstrous wave of contamination, entire tribes became extinct. Hospitable, simple people and their untarnished cultures were annihilated. Any strategy of education, relocation, and assimilation drawn up by the white settlers quickly became inconsequential as civilized disease spread like wildfire. It left thousands of dead tribes in its wake. The ancient knowledge, myth, and appreciation of life *and* death, which had always sustained them, died with them.

Our modern psychology finds it hard to put disease and harmful intentions together, but this is the primitive way. From the point of view of these natives, it is not the domestication of animals that causes pandemic diseases. The influence or intention of the people who brought them is what makes them sick. The intention always comes first. Our ancient man would go further and say that it *is* the disease. When cause and effect have not been separated and the intention *is* the action—as we discussed in Chapter 2—then in the case of colonial America, the greed was the disease, the dominance was the disease, and so forth.

Nowadays, we do not associate negative intention with illness. Long ago, we engineered a revolutionary social deception that we have also discussed: the ability to internalize the thoughts and feelings that drive us. Now we are able to exhibit behaviour that expresses something to the contrary. In primitive terms, this amounts to no less than sorcery. Time has seen to it that we have not retained any memory of having expressed ourselves in any other way. Our actions and our words are now far more real than whatever drives them. Non-primitive secondary emotions such as resentment, humiliation, pride, and shame also affect our ability to interpret the facts as they are. These are obstacles that psychotherapists and psychiatrists often find themselves navigating when dealing with mental illness. But from a primitive perspective, these thoughts and feelings do not only affect us mentally. As individuals, we have become such effective storage containers that our ability to conceal our intentions, plus a host of complex and confused emotions, is now a process of machine-like refinement. We now pass on this ability to our children through our genes. Consequently, it has become ridiculous to say that someone has cancer because they are harbouring resentment or anger, as much as it is to say that someone is obese because they are greedy. We accept that these problems are caused by what is happening solely in our bodies. Diet, surgery, and medication are the only reasonable solutions. To change our attitude, to address feelings that may be stuck, to say No! to the influences that feed off our needs and desires, are no longer viable options. We are living in a reality that is underpinned by a deception that means we never have to question what is happening in our inner worlds. After all, how can we be honest and clear about something we have trained ourselves not to see and so can legitimately ignore or deny?

From a primitive point of view, egocentricity and denial of this kind are dangerous and will have a devastating impact on our health. We are not accustomed to associating mental and physical illness with the development of this personal universe. But in a primitive world, if we entertain shadows, then disease, whether in the body or the mind, is inevitable. When we separate the physical affliction from our psychology, we are upholding the illusion that the physical component of life is all we need to address in order to stay healthy.

Our ancient man knows nothing of the horrors of modern illness as he basks in his simplicity. As far as he is concerned, the physical flaws we suffer are the result of having slowly disengaged from primitive values over many generations. For him, disease is a physical manifestation of what happens to our spirit when it is eaten away by something negative that we have learned to conceal. As he stands upon his mountain, he hardly knows what disease is. He has nowhere to harbour the intentions and feelings that cause it, even if he had the will to do so. But should he ever demonstrate that will, the rest of his people would be quick to 'deal' with him.

The humane genome

In 2012, science reported some interesting advancements in human DNA research that revealed new information about how our genes relate to the diseases that we suffer from today. Project Encode is a public research project launched by the U.S. National Human Genome Research Institute in September 2003. According to Encode, the human genome is packed with roughly four million switches that reside in about eighty per cent of our DNA. Researchers have discovered that these switches work as if they are part of an enormous control panel. It turns out that what we thought previously to be junk DNA is having a significant effect on how our cells and tissue behave. Subtle influences from the environment affect these switches, turning them on and triggering a specific disease. They have linked the switches to hundreds of illnesses including cancer, multiple sclerosis, Crohn's, and celiac disease. This discovery helps us to understand, among other things, why we get some diseases and not others. It also explains why identical twins do not get the same ones.

Encode tells us that fatal and debilitating diseases are lying dormant in our genes as they wait for something to trigger a switch. What the catalysts are exactly they have yet to find out, so the research does not help to prevent disease, only to explain it. So, if it is the case that a switch for turning cancer on exists in *all* our genes, why don't the African Bushmen get cancer? Why don't the Amazonian Pirahãs suffer from Parkinson's disease? Why don't we see primitive tribal people suffering from Alzheimer's or any of the astonishing 400 diseases that the scientists have identified within this panel of switches? In an attempt to answer these questions, we need to first distinguish between the types of disease that civilized and primitive people are susceptible to.

When illness occurs in primitive individuals, it is usually an assault from the environment in the form of pathogens. These are infectious agents such as viruses, bacteria, fungi or parasites that cause diseases in a host. They are afflictions that are caught, like a cold, or imposed, like malaria. Unlike us, primitive people are unable to elicit a disease *from the inside*, such as cancer, heart disease or Alzheimer's. If we think with a primitive mind, then we might assume that this is because tribal people have no inside within which to cultivate these diseases, just as there is nowhere for them to hide their thoughts and feelings.

On the other hand, primitive people understand mesmerism. The word *influenza* comes from the old French *influence*, 'to be mesmerized by the power of the stars'. Stars and the heavens have reigned over physical and mental health throughout time and various cultures the world over. In many primitive cultures (including the !Kung Bushmen), falling stars and meteor showers are powerful omens of death. In Western culture, if we attach any credence to a falling star other than what is scientific, it is usually to make a wish. What many of us do not take into account is that the wish-making (the part of the superstition we acknowledge) is inextricably linked to the star being an omen of death (the part of the superstition we conveniently disregard). In myth, when someone witnesses a falling star the influence in the heavens is strong, and they would be worried about what is going on at the time it occurs. There is no time to make a wish. The conditions in the stars when they fall to Earth are such that the heavens will make good the observer's desires at that very moment, positive or negative. It is this lack of control over omens and otherworldly events that relates to primitive ideas around destiny and luck. It also inspires primitive people to behave themselves. Witnessing a falling a star would not bode well for an ancient person, so what may follow it would more likely be a prayer than a wish.

According to the legend of the genie and his lamp, wishes come at a price. In this myth, we meet the formidable Middle Eastern *djinn* spirits. They are also associated with the stars and in particular the constellation of Orion. The *djinn* are powerful starry cave dwellers and renowned for educating ignorant mortals in the nature of values and principles. If we want something, what are we going to give up in return? The law states there must be an exchange. Are we prepared to allow a death to occur? Without a death, the birth of something new cannot take place. Those who take the genie's three wishes without honouring the sacrifice will bring bad luck and trouble to their lives, which may include sickness. Influence affects primitive and ancient people, whether it is psychological or physical. The stars can mesmerize tribal people. They can die from the common cold. But they cannot 'make' cancer.

So, where does all this leave the genes, cells, and DNA of our ancient man? Do the environmental influences that trigger these new switches reside solely within a civilized territory? Is Project Encode telling us that the conditions of the modern world are so appalling that they alone are the catalysts for 400 diseases that are otherwise dormant in our million-year-old man? Or, perhaps our ancient man's DNA does not contain the panel of switches because he has no genes, cells or DNA in the first place.

Ancestral building blocks

It appears that we have been trapped once again by a linear sequence of eureka moments. These are the links in the chain of scientific discovery that exist in the primitive dimension in their complete form. In isolation, these eureka moments tell us nothing about the bigger picture of life. We are again blind to the beginning and the end of the epic story, which we have talked about before. We are building an entire world from what we have gleaned from that one tiny random page we hold in our hands. We need to visit the ball of bread dough again.

These scientific discoveries that take decades of research to unveil, one discovery at a time, are perpetuating the illusion that the physical world is the only true reality. They do not consider that it is a reality that we have created, or that has been created by someone or something for reasons we have not yet looked into. It is feasible, therefore, that we have invented genes, genomes, and DNA to fit with the idea that the world is entirely physical simply because this is the way that we are currently choosing to see it. Let us consider again that we are living in an ancestor simulation. The program's designer will only present the microscopic details of our environment at a time when we become curious about those details and require an explanation. The program's architect will then design the explanation in line with where he or she is taking the program next. Nick Bostrom, Professor of Philosophy at Oxford University and Director of the Future of Humanity Institute, points out:

> '...a posthuman simulator would have enough computing power to keep track of the detailed belief-states in all human brains at all times. Therefore, when it saw that a human was about to make an observation of the microscopic world, it could fill in sufficient detail in the simulation in the appropriate domain on an as-needed basis.' (2003)

Either way, we know that modern diseases were absent from our ancient man's life. They could not exist for him because the principles upon which they exist are forbidden in his world. We also know that his parents did not pass defective genes on to him that predispose him to certain diseases. This could be because his physical form is such that genes are not part of his anatomy. So, when we examine Neanderthal DNA that we extract from fossils, what do we think we are looking at if Neanderthals did not have any DNA? When scientists claim they have sequenced a Neanderthal genome, what does that mean to the Neanderthal herself who did not actually have a genome? What are we looking at in ourselves when we say two per cent or so of our DNA relates to our Neanderthal cousins? Where were *their* dormant diseases and switches?

The building blocks of our ancient man and the Neanderthal people were made from something distinctly different: ancestral memory. Their version of a genetic code consisted of millions of years of ancestral knowledge, just as it does for an oak tree, a crocodile or a honeybee. It is their ancestors and the language of animism that dictate instructions on how to live, grow and die, and not to change. Modern people have separated the directives regarding human life into two camps: science and religion. We have one instruction manual for the physical aspect, another for the spiritual, and while they both battle for supremacy, neither of them addresses the part of life that affects us most of all: society. On the other hand, primitive ancestral knowledge encompasses all these elements, so there is no need for biology, theology or sociology. From the perspective of our ancient man, biology consists of images or mental impressions, ancient memory or knowledge, and tribal social values. These elements have materialized in the modern civilized dimension via their own collapse. So when we study the genetic code of a Neanderthal, we are looking at ancient memory that has been measured.

Lest we forget

How and when did *Homo sapiens* manage to lose or forget the instructions on what to do when transformation looms? We find clues to the answer to this question in the changes that occurred in the prehistoric rituals around death, in particular, the introduction of intentional and ceremonial burial. Pervasive changes in attitude and behaviour took place around the world within a period called the Aurignacian period, 45,000 to 25,000 years ago. Before our ancestors started to bury people, we assume that people's bodies were left out for the animals and birds when they died.

This period when intentional burial was significantly taken up by humans denotes the beginning of a marked transition away from a primitive existence. Somewhat abruptly, death started to attract a lot of strange attention that many experts in prehistoric religion account for in terms of a spiritual revolution. Some say we were adapting to climate change, others that we were establishing ideas about power and status by burying certain important individuals. Most seem to discuss it with a degree of evolutionary inevitability. We, however, will not. We will view the changes around death and spirituality as developments that were not unavoidable. We will consider that significant life changes were engineered and imposed upon primitive people who had no idea what spiritual, in a religious sense, meant. The cycle of birth, growth, and death had been comfortably ticking along for millions of years. The primitive mindset of animism, ancestors, and spirit persons is not a religious doctrine that is attached to their everyday life. It *is* everyday life. So what was happening to these people that initiated such drastic changes in their ritual behaviour?

What we start to see in terms of the archaeology is intentional burials appearing in numbers we have not seen before. Also, we find people interred with grave goods or in an odd manner, such as without their heads, with a mysterious extra limb or with animal bones strategically placed on certain parts of the body. There were many factors involved that are confusing and hard to explain. Burial during this time was still quite rare in that communities only dealt with a select few in this way. For this reason, archaeologists assume that it was a privilege, that the act of burial and the inclusion of any amount of grave goods suggest the individuals were important. But this assumption rests itself on more recent human behaviour. Burial of any kind 50,000 years ago was a sporadic operation executed by primitive hunter-gatherers with no obvious intention. This is in contrast to the much later Neolithic and Bronze Age burials. Once the Neolithic Revolution was underway, prestigious burial mounds and grand stone tombs became commonplace. Burials during this time were clearly status-oriented as established social hierarchies and elitism were fully operational. But this was not the case 50,000 years ago. So what was happening in the lives of these egalitarian hunters to make them behave in this radical new way? We need to look at the way extant tribal people handle death to appreciate how peculiar this behaviour is.

We have already touched upon the way tribes do not formalize death by way of ceremony and solemnity. The primitive way is to openly grieve, which usually involves loud wailing and crying. Thereafter, it is important to make sure the spirit of the deceased moves on and does not linger in a ghostly way around those who are still living.

Lorna J. Marshall in her remarkable ethnographic text *Nyae Nyae !Kung: Beliefs and Rites* talks about rituals performed by the !Kung Bushmen and their primitive attitude toward death. She says, 'We did not find highly developed rites performed for death and burial among the !Kung', and that 'their purpose for burying the dead was to keep carnivores from eating the corpse and to cover the smell of decaying flesh.' This is the typical ceremony-free, down-to-earth, primitive attitude that we find in tribes around the world today. Of the utmost importance to tribal, nomadic people, including the Bushmen, is to ensure that the spirit of the deceased is not tempted to stay around the camp. If they do, they will bring bad luck and sickness to the tribe. For this reason, the !Kung move their camp a little way from the spot of a recent burial to ensure the deceased is not disturbed. Before they move, they ritually put out their campfire and relight it in the new camp. They will mark the grave with small stones so people passing will know not to disturb the spirit by walking on it. Then, the grave must be left alone: '...if a mortal should visit [the grave] often, the spirit of the dead might take notice and wonder why that person was there. The spirit might become displeased and do something harmful to the person.' The Bushmen also cover the grave with thorny branches from trees and bushes to stop animals trying to dig up the corpse to eat it. Thorn bushes are also protective in traditional Romani culture, but in this case it was to prevent the spirit or ghost of the deceased from getting out and terrorizing the tribe! There are many stories of primitive and nomadic people prohibiting activities around a death that might encourage the spirit of the deceased to linger and bring misfortune to the clan.

There are other Romani Gypsy customs similar to some of the primitive tribal traditions we find around the world. For instance, they must not utter the name of someone who has died for at least a year[3] (the Bushmen and Pirahãs also do this), their favourite dinner will *not* be cooked in case they decide to join you to eat it, and all their belongings including their *vardo* (caravan) are set on fire. This may sound a little extreme but there are many examples of tribal customs where personal items belonging to the deceased are wrecked and thrown away. Arrows of hunters are snapped in half, objects considered to have the spirit of the one who has died within them are destroyed. This helps the spirit of the deceased to move on and encourages good luck within the tribe.

These primitive rituals are to encourage the spirit to continue on to wherever it needs to go. They are not solely for the benefit of loved ones who remain. Primitive people believe it to be considerate to those who have died if they help them to move on by demonstrating—through ritual—that they should. By removing the things the deceased was attached to, the tribe is helping them through the transformation. It also helps those who are grieving to let them go.

We could not have a more contrasting attitude to death and burial in Western life today. Apart from visiting the graves of those we have lost on a regular basis, we also annually read out the names of those who die in disasters such as 9/11. We might leave someone's room or entire house untouched and enshrined with their personal things, as if they are about to walk back in at any moment or as if they are still there! Primitive

---

[3] If you shared the name of the deceased you may well be required to change it for that time.

people are likely to think such rituals would aggravate the spirits of the deceased. This is not a good idea seeing as they have entered the otherworld and will have acquired power and influence that they can wield over mortals who annoy them. These modern rituals are also troubling to primitive people for another reason. Visiting graves, setting up shrines and honouring anniversaries are activities that encourage the spirits of those who have died to linger around the place of death. Many primitive tribes believe that once we die we are in the hands of ancestors. When we have let go of life and untied ourselves from 'here', we qualify to return now and then as the spirit of an ancestor who guides and encourages those who remain here. If someone stays shackled to Earth after death through a memory of trauma, guilt, obligation or any other concern that prevents them from letting go (such as their favourite dinner), they will become stuck. They will be a ghost haunting that place and bad luck and sickness will in turn affect the people who live there. Enacting rituals to help those who have died to move on is another example of the way tribespeople act to prevent negative influences from entering their lives. They are covering another loophole.

There is a link between the primitive obsession with avoiding ghosts or zombies and their nomadic lifestyle. To be a ghost means that the spirit or life force is stuck in some way because a transformation is not complete. In psychological terms, this can also apply when we are still alive. If our minds fix us to a physical place or a person, or the memory of an ordeal from the past overwhelms us, life will stagnate like water in a dead pool.

We could say that the nomadic mindset is not 'to move around' but 'not to be stuck'.

Life before the afterlife

So what occurred all that time ago in prehistory that led to Western people no longer understanding death in this practical way? What provoked such a dramatic change that we are now unable to let go of our loved ones without feeling guilty or obligated? Our mindset today generally regards the liberation from grief as disrespectful to those who have died. We certainly do not consider that without the courage to free ourselves from our grief we are in danger of encouraging our loved ones to live around us as ghosts.

Our million-year-old man knows about death and letting go. In his dimension, he is sensitive to the cycle of life and death *because* he is primitive not despite it. When someone he loves dies, it is difficult and challenging. With support from his tribe he ritualizes his grief through which he releases the spirit of the person who has died. He does not act this out ceremonially. It is an emotional expression, an outpouring, and then it is gone. Everyday life continues once it is over.

Experiencing a death in this simple way helps people's thoughts and emotions to flow freely and not stagnate. The reward that follows this process, whereby our ancient man is able to return to his everyday life without a heavy heart, is forsaken by modern people who feel compelled to hold on. We often hear of mothers, fathers, widows, siblings, sons, and daughters living in torment years after their loved ones have passed, instead of letting them go and feeling liberated. A primitive community helps individuals who may be stuck in this way to find the strength to move on. But in the West we wrap them in blankets of sentimentality, which only prolongs the sorrow.

When someone we love dies, it is a painful experience. We can go to pieces, and it might take a long time to put those pieces back together again. Primitive people also feel the loss acutely. We hear it in their gut-wrenching wails, we see it in their collapsing bodies and in their tears of despair. But their grief cannot last. As a ritual, they express it completely as there is nowhere for them to store the feelings. Through their dramatic expression, the deceased is dispatched to the otherworld. Many tribes believe this is an act of kindness because no one wants to end up as a ghost when they die. Some say loud wailing encourages the spirit to move on, and many ancient cultures considered the act of grieving to be an art. For this reason, we still find professional mourners in parts of China and Asia. A heartfelt wail can catapult the spirit of someone who has died away from the land of the living. It also helps other friends and family members to connect with their grief. Drumming, singing, and chanting at funerals are also approved of. Religious silence and solemn faces are sure signs that ghosts will be lurking.

So, if we return then to the appearance of the strange burial practices of our Stone Age ancestors and consider death from this robust and down-to-earth perspective, it seems we have a problem. The introduction of odd rituals around death, such as removing heads and adding limbs, indicates that these ancient people were responding to something new and jarring that they had not experienced before. Contrary to what some experts believe, I don't think it was a change in the weather.

Many writers of ancient culture and belief talk about this period 50,000 years ago as a time when people were becoming aware of death and mortality. The new burials and the accompanying ceremonies are signs that our ancestors were adopting a religious attitude. Experts believe that alongside the development of the human intellect and the conscious mind, ancient people were conceiving the dimension we call the afterlife. They were starting to concern themselves with heaven, the soul, and everlasting life.

This account of spiritual awakening suggests that these burial rites are then evidence of the root of dualism—the perception of 'the self' and 'the other'. It insinuates that before our ancestors started burying people, their lives were purely physical and utilitarian. We assume that finding no evidence of ceremony means belief systems, gods, and religious sentiments were absent. However, primitive people in the world today, whose otherworld is as large as life and whose ancestral realm is alive and well, demonstrate that this cannot be the case. The primitive perception of animism and spirit persons is a perception that keeps an entire system of life intact. It is not religious because it is not dualistic. It is not ceremonial. It is a mindset. But the idea of life without religion that is *not* fundamentally physical is an alien concept within civilized thinking. This is because we cannot imagine a scenario where the material world is not our main focus of attention. Civilized religion, therefore, involves attaching a mysterious and ethereal dimension to our 'real' everyday world. In a primitive dimension, the everyday world is merely brought to life. The otherworld is with them constantly. The rocks and trees and sky are not dead things, just as people who have died are not extinguished. The vitality of life travels in and out of everything like a flowing river or a blowing wind. It does not travel from 'here' to 'there'.

Weston La Barre, author of *Ghost Dance: The Origins of Religion,* describes new rituals within a society as cults developing out of trauma. He says, 'there can be no cult without crisis,' and that social trauma leads to a search for the 'revitalization' of a lost collective harmony. From this perspective, marked changes in cultural and ritual behaviour, such as those we are looking at, are not conscious developments into something new. They are examples of how people take action in an attempt to return to something original that has been disrupted. If life is unable to return to the way it was, then what we might call 'cultural evolution' is born. New rituals and behaviour that become standardized over time are the unintentional result of trying to reinstate what was once normal within a community.

Considering this, it becomes clear that these strange new religious acts are ritualistic responses to something that was happening *to* them. When we take into account the primitive psychology of these ancient people and the animistic and repetitive nature of their behaviour, this theory becomes even more feasible. The strange nature of the burials and the suddenness of their appearance suggest they are the result of an imposed disturbance. Factors that are unknown to us were upsetting the natural integrity of their world and the usually untroubled process of dying and death. These new rituals then provide a visible marker for us in the archaeology, which we interpret *incorrectly* as evidence of a new spiritual awareness. Prior to this, there is no evidence and, therefore, no awareness. This mistaken interpretation then leads us to create *two* worlds—the physical world and the spiritual world. But this split is only according to our modern perspective because these people did not perceive two separate worlds, but one all-encompassing world. Therefore, this phenomenal behavioural revolution was not the result of a sudden collective epiphany, when mankind became aware and, therefore, fearful of his own mortality. It was clearly 'in opposition to', but in opposition to what?

As much as we can say that life after death was becoming of interest to our ancestors, we can also say that by extracting the afterlife from its rightful place in the otherworld the material world intensified as it became estranged from its otherworldly counterpart. Could it be that there are beings living in the primitive otherworld who are looking at this division from the other side of the fence? Perhaps there are people with a different perception of reality to ours who ridicule the idea of a physical world simply because they cannot see it. This separation of spirit and matter over time may not have created the material world, but it has fuelled our infatuation with it. This becomes clearer thousands of years later during the Neolithic Revolution when the process of civilizing began. At this point in the story though, we will assume that these new burial rites were not an evolutionary step towards spirituality or religion. We will view them as a psychological and behavioural response to something out of the ordinary that we are about to explore.

CHAPTER 8

Dimensional Thresholds

'She looked back over her shoulder and there, between the dark tree
trunks, she could see the open doorway of the wardrobe and even
catch a glimpse of the empty room from which she had set out.'
C S Lewis

The events in prehistory that altered the way we handle death relate to the way we manage and perceive life and death in modern times. They hold a key to the puzzle regarding how we have changed so drastically that as a species we no longer resemble anything our million-year-old man would recognize. The strange death rituals that began around 50,000 years ago represent a shift in a vital primitive process: transformation. This is a process that transports us from one place to another.

In the more modern arena of spiritual understanding and teaching, particularly in the East, we find transformation is a fundamental property of life. It is a basic principle among some of the ancient Eastern religions such as Taoism and Buddhism. Texts such as the Taoist *Chuang-tzu* refer to the 'constant flow of transformation and change'. The Eastern mystics regard the continual movement within the timeless dynamic of the universe as an intuitive wisdom that we are integral to. They do not measure life with the ruler of time, space, and conscious rationality. The transformative process is an essential component of the cycle of creation, preservation, and destruction, and the primitive birth, growth, and death cycle, which we met in Chapter 4. It is the element that allows these cycles of life to function because it keeps everything flowing smoothly. However, we rarely associate the wisdom of these old religions with ancient hunter-gatherers. Although they revere simplicity and discourage material desires just as in tribal life, it is an intellectual far-sightedness and not a primitive instinct that accompanies this simplicity. The Eastern mystic promotes a refinement of the mind and encourages the careful management of thoughts and ideas. This entails a regular emptying and cleansing of the conscious container that the process of civilizing has created. But the container remains nonetheless.

It is, however, primitive individuals with container-less animal-like minds who will act out this life of intuition, instinct, and oneness with nature that the old religions talk about. They live in this way because they can do nothing else. Their natural integrity makes them immune to conscious influence. They live with no religious undertones, and any sanctity is in their relationship with the natural world and the domestic harmony of their clan. They are unable to break from that format. The transformational nature of our ancient man is instinctive and ritualistic. It underpins everything he does, just as the transformative seasons underpin everything in nature. We do not associate his delicate simplicity with wisdom because what he knows he does not speak of. The primitive *integrity principle* means he cannot speak of that which he is a part otherwise he is *apart,* and his world would collapse.

Although our ancient man does not change in the sense that he does not evolve, he does transform throughout his life, just as we see nature transforming throughout the year. His initiation at the onset of puberty, when he makes his first kill in the hunt, when he marries, when his children are born, when family members die, and of course when he dies—these are all challenging events that transform him and lead him to maturity. These transformations in primitive life are of the utmost importance. The celebrations that continue to surround them today in most tribal communities are evidence of that. They are marking the completion of an individual's transition, which is sometimes subtle, perhaps even unnoticeable to modern eyes and ears.

To appreciate the relevance of these events, it is useful to look again at the two transformational experiences that we have explored: death and ostracism. Each process starts with us feeling challenged, either because someone has died or because our clan has shut us out. These events then prompt us to search for the qualities that will take us through the experience. With death, we need to let go of someone we love. With ostracism, we need to relinquish whatever behaviour led to our exclusion. Initially, we feel discomfort in the form of frustration, anxiety, fear or grief. But if we take action and we let go then we are relieved. The end result is that the transformation rewards us with a *value* instead of a *memory*. The former takes us forward into maturity, and the latter takes us back to the past. In practice, primitive transformation is a simple process, but nonetheless an essential psychological component of the workings of primitive life.

The Pirahãs aid this process by giving themselves a new name to mark the occasion. It draws a clear line across the seam for everyone to acknowledge and allows them to move through life learning from their experience without holding on to it. The name change is a loophole ritual, like when Romani Gypsies do not mention the name of someone who has died. It stops people from worrying about the past. The transformational process will break down if we are stuck in the past. Many tribal people do not have the same name all their lives in the way we do. They change them according to what is happening to them. In some cases, the tribe gives them a name. Others have no name at all.

Invisible doorways

When we talk about transformation, we are talking about the transition between one state and another. Between those states, there is a period of *non*-state. In this state, we feel as if we are *going through something* because we experience a sense of motion as we travel from where we are now to a new destination. In the primeval dimension where there is no geography, this is the closest we come to travelling distance. This non- or in-between-state is what we will refer to as a portal. As we know, portals relate to seams. Seams are times and places that depict something ending and something else beginning, such as at dawn or dusk. A portal *contains* the transformational experience. A seam is a set of circumstances that allow the experience to occur.

Quantum physics provides an interesting backdrop for exploring the existence of portals. To be able to apply this backdrop, we again have to try removing the physical conditioning we carry around with us. Our minds need to imagine taking away all the weight, distance, geography, and time we are so familiar with, as well as the linearity we apply to our thoughts and experience. If we imagine our ancient man who lives without these things as having the qualities of a computer, it is easier to envisage a world where portals exist as a normal part of the journey through life. In his world, there are invisible doorways acting as gates, through which he can travel from one environment to another via the process of transformation. This process is like the electrical current that travels through a logic gate in a computer circuit. Time and space, distance, geography, and consciousness have no part to play.

Within the regions of outer space, we accept the theory of wormholes. Wormholes are hypothetical shortcuts through space-time. They enable instantaneous passage from one place to another without having to experience any geography or distance that might otherwise be involved. Of course, we cannot do this in practice because of the restrictions imposed by our three dimensions. Our fixation with measurement and the separation of 'us' from everything else means dimensional travel is impossible. But we know our ancient man did not live in a measured universe, so we can assume that, in principle, wormholes and portals of a digital quality were a usual part of life for him. We also find these portals in ancient myths.

There are mythical portals and gateways to other worlds and dimensions in stories within almost every ancient culture. Ancient Rome had a god of doorways—*Janus*. He was the patron of beginnings and endings and the origin of the word January as he represented the huge gateway through to the new solar year. The word *Janus* is also connected to *travelling* or *passing*, as in the Sanskrit word *yanah*. To ancient people, doorways were powerful, symbolic representations of the seams between worlds.

The ancient Sumerian story *The Epic of Gilgamesh* is one of the earliest stories to have survived the passage of time. In it we find dreams, dimensions, and timelessness enveloping a tragic story of the death of primeval, wild strength and the birth of human mortality. In life, Enkidu the wild man and his civilized counterpart Gilgamesh come together as brothers and act as renegades against the otherworld. They chop down an ancient pine forest after killing its guardian. They kill the sacred Bull of Heaven that the great god Anu had sent to discipline them. Both events depict the transition to civilized values by way of the wilful destruction of a magical otherworld. Unfortunately for Enkidu, his primitive innocence makes him vulnerable to the pressure put upon him by the angry gods. The strain caused by alien feelings of guilt and remorse is too much for him, and he dies. Gilgamesh is grief-stricken by the death of his friend. He leaves the city and takes off into the countryside where he comes to a mountain guarded by giant scorpion men. They are protecting the path through to the land of the sun, they 'guard its gate...they guard the sun at dawn and dusk'. Gilgamesh demands to be let through and the scorpion men warn him, "It is impossible, Gilgamesh, nobody has passed through the mountain's inaccessible tract. For even after twelve leagues the darkness is too dense, there is no light." Driven by his pain and grief, Gilgamesh attempts the journey through this mythical portal. At the end, exhausted and wretched, he 'came out in front of the sun...brightness was everywhere...bushes were visible, blossoming with gemstones'. He had transformed.

In the modern world, there are invisible portals and seams too. While there are hundreds of doorways, entrances, and exits that we can see and physically walk through, there are also hidden ones. An example is that which separates the dimensions of the everyday physical world and the minute world of quantum physics. Between these two distinct worlds, there is a hidden seam. We will pass through the portal that relates to this seam only when we work out how to unify the laws of the two worlds. This enigma appears in the corner of our eye. It is an image dancing in our peripheral vision, and as we turn to look at it, it disappears. We feel its presence, but our limited understanding of how the universe works prevents us from looking directly upon it. The invisible quantum universe surrounds us. It is in the air, within every atom of the chair I am sitting on, and in the starlight that shines upon the world on a clear night. The primeval universe also surrounds us. It is in every leaf upon every tree, within the sunlight, and in the tiniest grain of sand on a beach. The principles behind both these so-called worlds are available to us at any time, yet our interaction with them *on their terms* is irritatingly restricted. If we could find the door to the quantum nanoworld and travel through it, we might discover it is like walking into Dr Who's Tardis. It may not be tiny at all, but far greater than our clumsy, measured world because it exists outside the restrictions that those measurements impose. After all, it is the act of measuring that prevents us from crossing dimensions in the first place. Perhaps we would find that the quantum and primeval worlds are not two worlds but the same world.

As with the door to the ostracized dimension, this portal is not visible to the physical eye. These gateways only appear when experience and circumstance amount to their creation, and we adjust our senses to perceive them. Then, we search for the qualities required to travel through the experience and it transports us—as through a wormhole—to a completely different landscape, just like Gilgamesh. The transformation takes us somewhere new even though we have not travelled any distance at all.

The problems we encounter with this scenario are again due to the way the laws of our three-dimensional reality state that there is distance between us and everything else in the universe. This linearity within space fixes us in the 'and' of 'cause and effect'. But the truth is that distance lies only in our *perception* of space. In a primitive world, any concept of distance would not involve physical travelling at all, just like the operations in a computer. As quantum scientist Caslav Brukner pointed out during his experiments with *entanglement* and causality a few years ago, causal order is *not* a fundamental property of nature. In the primeval dimension, our ancient man would agree.

When he looks at the stars, he is with the stars. When he looks at the moon, he is with her and she is with him; they are together. His innate ability to relate to everything, his intentions, senses, and emotions are what drive him to a place.

As we have already discussed, mathematical processes and principles exist in a primeval world. Our ancient man understands the principles of a computer even though he has never seen one. He knows how to travel to the stars. Timelessness and dimensional travel are all quite normal for him. But stuck in the passage of time as we are, or in the 'and' of cause and effect, we have to discover the facts of life in a succession of steps. We exacerbate this scenario by devoting our lives to our physical actions, instead of feeling driven by qualities and principles that we merely demonstrate or ritualize within those activities.

From a primitive perspective, the portals between worlds are not out of the ordinary. It is the primitive laws and the way we express them using ritual that are key to knowing where those portals are and how to travel through them. It turns out to be our devout trust in materialism that has led us to dismiss this primitive element of life as if it is unimportant. Any relationship with nature has become irrelevant with regard to how we approach the structure of our lives. How we relate to each other and the environment, develop social networks, and study the world we live in, which includes quantum physics, have nothing to do with primitive values. But our million-year-old man says that our relationship with primitive nature *is* quantum physics. It is where we will find the answer to the frustrating problem of dimensional travel, *decoherence* and collapse.

Now you see me, now you don't

With all this in mind, let us look again at the revolution that took place in Palaeolithic prehistory. For years, archaeologists, anthropologists, and prehistorians have puzzled over these massive cultural changes. The introduction of ceremonial burial, along with the Cro-Magnon[4] cave art of around a similar time, continues to mystify us. As primitive psychologists, we are particularly interested in terms of how extreme the psychological changes were that enabled this behaviour to develop. Concepts were starting to take hold in the mindset of people who should not have been able to conceptualize. The revolutionary establishment of agriculture some 35,000 years later marks the height of these changes, the pinnacle of the perceptual revolution that had led up to it. In modern times, we tend to reflect upon the Neolithic Revolution as the age when civilization began, but it was also the end of an age. Millions of years of natural, instinctive freedom within a social and environmental integrity were dramatically concluded when humans started farming. The disruption began with ceremonial burials and art, and it ended with agriculture. This is the context within which we are looking at this massive shift.

So who were these extraordinary modern humans who appeared out of nowhere around 50,000 years ago? As we are not travelling an evolutionary road within this story, we can safely say that these people did not evolve from our simple, ancient

---

[4] Cro-Magnon is a subspecies of *Homo sapiens* and formally known as Early European Modern Humans (EEMH).The name 'Cro-Magnon' refers to the rock shelter in southwest France where they were first found in the nineteenth century.

man whose quantum integrity makes him immune to change anyway.

It is not enough to say that environmental catalysts alone initiated the sensational developments in the *Homo sapiens* genus such as we see in the Cro-Magnon people. Their culture—the Aurignacian tool culture—demonstrated extraordinary sophistication in terms of blade technology, hunting, art, home-making, and, of course, elaborate burials. All of a sudden and very quickly these people dispersed across a large part of the world. While it took 200,000 years for *Homo sapiens* to plod across Africa, by the time we reach 45,000 years ago, these early modern humans raced across the Near East and Europe in less than 20,000 years.

Such swift passage, superior technology and methods of hunting are intriguing. What is also interesting about this period is that we do not find Neanderthals, the indigenous people of the Near East and Europe, changing at all. In general, the Neanderthals did not adopt any of the techniques introduced by these people because their ritualistic lifestyle would not have allowed foreign knowledge to compromise their social relationships. Any small signs archaeologists might find to suggest otherwise will more likely be due to the presence of someone sophisticated in the vicinity. It is possible that some Neanderthals were 'adopted' by Cro-Magnon clans, forced to breed, and join in with behaviour that they would not have understood. Otherwise, they carried on just as they were for a brief period until they died out. They had completely disappeared by about 40,000 years ago. The debate over whether or not *Homo sapiens* murdered, assimilated or out-competed the Neanderthals is still ongoing among experts. Probably all three are true to some extent. It is also likely that their birth rates would have diminished as their familiar ritualized lifestyle was put under pressure. There are minimal signs of conflict between *Homo sapiens* and Neanderthals in the archaeology. This suggests that Neanderthals were not warring people but more like wild animals—predictable, easily frightened, and quick to run away. Their physical hardiness did not necessarily make them good warriors because if they met with conflict that was outside their usual ritual behaviour they would not have understood the situation. They would not have known what to do. This is hard for a modern mind to imagine, as it is usual for us to quickly analyze a situation and modify our behaviour accordingly. And of course, conflict and war are sadly now second nature to us. But 'wrestling' large animals is where Neanderthals demonstrated immense strength, courage, directness, and other values *ritualistically*. Primitive conflict or combat has little to do with brute force and more to do with the demonstration of qualities and relationships in the form of what we would consider to be repetitive, unconscious behaviour. They would never before have met with the concept of *non-ritualized* behaviour, a factor that I believe is at the root of their extinction. Rather like the polar bear, the giant panda, and other wild animals are unable to evolve so they might survive the changes we impose on their lives, Neanderthals could not survive the changes that the Cro-Magnons made to theirs.

The Neanderthal people are a wonderful example of a fundamental point of this book: primitive humans are not designed to change. Their unbending allegiance to the natural world is where we find their extraordinary intelligence. They demonstrate to us that human life in its original form is not about winning biological competitions. It does not involve developing and changing. It is about staying in tune with the primitive laws of their species and the world around them, regardless of what changes are taking place. Neanderthals never betrayed the natural boundaries of their species, but were fatally caught up with those who did. From this perspective, these new and sophisticated *Homo sapiens* were alarmingly different.

When we disregard the evolutionary timeline, we are free to investigate different theories about the way people came and went from this place we call Earth. We know that throughout this timeline, there were people who appeared suddenly and then disappeared just as quickly, and the only headache we have is arranging them in the obligatory linear format. There are other examples of prehistoric humans like the Cro-Magnon people, where we have little or no evidence of the developmental phases that led up to their appearance. *Homo floresiensis*, also known as 'hobbits', were a metre-high Stone Age people who lived in caves on an island in Indonesia. These astonishing humans date back to at least 38,000 years ago and experts believe them to be a species distinct from *Homo sapiens* due to their size and ape-like bone and joint development.

Another unexplainable human apparition is the Clovis culture of North America. For many years, experts believed that the Clovis people were the first humans to colonize the Americas. Attributed to the *Homo sapiens* species, they were craftsmen of distinctively shaped flint arrows and tools known as the Clovis point. They used a technique of fluting the points that we do not find anywhere else in the world. They appeared with nothing preceding them around 13,000 BCE and disappeared again a few thousand years later. Eighty per cent of the North American wildlife, such as mammoth, mastodon, and giant sloth, also disappeared around this time. Experts sometimes refer to this period as the 'big-game extinction of North America', but they do not know what caused it. They cannot hold man or climate responsible for the extinction of an unbelievable thirty-five genera of animals around this time.

The page of the evolutionary story that includes our ancient axeman is also rather blank. We cannot accredit *Homo ergaster* to any ancestral *Homo* line with confidence. Where he came from and what became of him is still in question. What we do know is that during his phenomenal amount of time on Earth, he and his stunning axe did not change.

The archaeology tells us that people and animals were appearing and disappearing from this dimension of Earth throughout time. In terms of a non-linear explanation, which is what interests us, Earth 50,000 years ago appears not as a planet but a layer of perception. It seems there were dimensions or 'layered realities' that these people travelled and frequented. They were able to travel to and from these layers because of their lighter physical form and their centred psychology. And, of course, three-dimensional space was an unknown concept. We must also consider that *the senses* were integral to how people perceived reality. We do not sense three-dimensional reality in the same way. We have it imposed upon us. It is solid and jarring. It is inflexible and irrefutable. Ours is a perceived reality that has been measured and so it has collapsed. Realities that have not collapsed would relate to one another by sharing principles based on a primitive ethos or universal natural laws. I believe Earth could have been a place like this a very long time ago.

Considering the penal colony theory, whereby nature and the wider universe have ostracized Earth and imprisoned it using physical laws, it is not hard to imagine that outside our confinement exists a multiverse teeming with life. In view of such a framework, we might also imagine 'people' travelling, or dimension-hopping, which would have included Earth as a destination before it collapsed. Within this hypothesis could be the root of 'sky gods' in traditional cultures. They would not have been 'gods' originally, nor 'ancient aliens' who came to teach the ignorant tribes of Earth how to civilize (we meet those in the next chapter). They were merely 'beings' who were visiting the indigenous people of Earth as if it was a normal part of life in the universe.

Ancient people could have known how to cross dimensions if portal technology involved the art of transformation and an integral relationship with the natural world. It is perhaps rational to consider mythical portals as analogies depicting symbols within a story. But there are so many references throughout cultures and across time that surely rational thinking cannot explain them all. There are creation myths that describe entire peoples emerging from caves, out of water or a hole in the ground. In an animistic world where physicality and evolution are invalid concepts, these mythical portals become examples of magnificent seams where influences are strong. Ancient people would have understood this and instinctively worked with these elements. Today, we have portals working invisibly in our computers. They demonstrate to us that this magical technology also exists in the material world and that we too have started to learn, or relearn, how to work with it. And our understanding of that technology is advancing all the time. If we take the myths from the beginning of time and the technology from the end of time, then we will have a quantum otherworld where there is no time at all. That is when we may find we can travel dimensions too.

The abrupt appearance of sophisticated (but still primitive) humans 50,000 years ago, plus the sudden obsession with portals, burial, and death, speak of fundamental changes taking place in our human world. Imagine, a cosmos full of activity, people crossing dimensions, somewhere time is not present and the seams between one place and another are traversable without distance. All sorts of ancient people may have been toing and froing like this for millions of years. And, we have established that the strange burial rituals are reminiscent of desperate people trying to rectify something that has gone wrong. Then, from such a perspective, it could look like this extraordinary process was breaking down. Cro-Magnon people no longer came and went as they may have been doing for millions of years—they *stayed*. It was not that they had evolved from the indigenous people here, but that they appeared on the scene and couldn't leave. The process of transformation had broken down. They had become stuck.

The Red Lady of Paviland is the earliest known ceremonial burial of a modern human in Britain, dating to approximately 33,000 BCE. She is in fact a he and his bones were found in a cave off the coast of Gower in South Wales in the nineteenth century. He had been buried with his body covered in red ochre, without his head, and with periwinkle shells and ivory rods placed upon him. His is a typical ceremonial burial by the Cro-Magnon people of this era.

In order for natural portals to work, they must be attached to a seam. A seam is a place or a time where something emerges from somewhere or where one thing leads to another. This explains why caves, such as that of the Red Lady, were a principal location in ancient times for art and burial. It also explains why the spirits of caves and mountains have power in the eyes of tribal people. It is possible that the process of transformation was breaking down for unknown reasons, and glitches in the technology were starting to appear. To begin with, the changes may have been subtle and erratic. After a while, these people may have found that the portal technology and the otherworld to which it belonged were slipping away, like a television that loses its signal. Another possibility is that someone—or something—was deliberately shutting it down from the other side.

Exit left

While we are talking about the burial of a physical body, it is useful to remind ourselves how we may have perceived our bodies in a primeval world. Similar to images in a vivid dream, our physique would be lightweight, perhaps faintly translucent, and, without having to travel the 'bits in between', would be direct and quick. In this way, their composition would not have comprised DNA and a genetic code, a brain or any other physical organs that would weigh the individual down. The weight we drag around with us now would not have existed, nor would the time it takes to act things out or get things done except in a ritualistic sense. Our bodies would be images that reflect our intentions, emotions, and personalities. We know the Neanderthals were physically strong and well-built, which reflected the robust character of their species and not just their physical abilities. Our ancient man was tall and slight, indicating that the character of his species was quick and sharp. These attributes reveal themselves in how he looks, but their roots are in his psychology and not his chromosomes. What, then, would happen to such an ethereal *non*-body when that person died? If they possessed the subtle form we have envisioned here, would they even die at all?

Let us imagine we are primitive and dying. We have come to the end of our life in a normal way, our family is around us, and we start to drift into a slumber. As if we are falling asleep, our physical awareness begins to wane, and our surroundings gradually diminish. The image of our body would simply behave in the same way; it also begins to fade. Eventually, it disappears completely, leaving nothing behind to bury or burn. If we have not collapsed into a three-dimensional material world—if we have not solidified—the qualities that make up who we are would return to their source leaving no sign that we were ever here.

Intentional burial in terms of the passage of time began significantly about 50,000 years ago. This behavioural change was caused by alterations to the way we experience physical reality. The quantum collapse—the solidification of a perceived life— appears to have begun at this time. Imagine experiencing this phenomenal change, from a sensuous world built from imagery and instinct to a world where those images start to gain weight. Our senses start to register a strange substance in and around certain places and things. The dreamlike images that have always surrounded us seem to be hardening. We can feel ourselves growing dense, as if our delicate form is being wrapped in layers of blankets that we cannot take off. Our quickness slows and sharpness dulls. This is the stuff of nightmares for a primitive mind. Imagine a loved one is dying. They are leaving this world for the other, but instead of fading away as we expect them to, a strange fleshy body is left behind, like a dinner guest might leave behind their coat at the end of an evening. For the first time, we have a corpse on our hands. The image has become an object, the essence a thing.

We could imagine that leaving our body on Earth when we died would be quite a shock for anyone who had never before been physical enough for it to happen. And once you have a dead body, what do you do with it? The incomplete nature of death in these circumstances might explain the fear of zombies that is prevalent in many tribal cultures. Considering their abhorrence of ghosts and zombies, ancient people may have thought that this new corpse would encourage the spirit of the deceased to linger. Having left an integral part of themselves in this world, they will find it hard to move on. The tribe may also have thought that spirits other than the corpse's owner might want to claim it in a vampiric way. I am presenting this theory as the flip side of the body and soul split. Prehistoric shamans with active imaginations did not suddenly become capable of religious ideology; they did not *invent* the otherworld as a welcome relief from the mundane. From a psychological point of view, that would be impossible. What seems to have happened is the opposite of what prehistorians tell us. The 'other' world within which people lived their everyday lives was collapsing in on itself. Time and three spatial dimensions were beginning to make an appearance, and our prehistoric ancestors were unable to reverse it. We are now imprisoned in this form, and it all began with the disruption of the transformational process and the formation of a corpse.

For the tribes that knew it was an omen of bad luck if individuals were not able to reach the ancestral realm when they died, this scenario is a horror story. But it could explain the burials where people have removed heads, taken bodies apart, rearranged bones, and introduced lucky charms. They would have hoped that these activities would confuse any loitering spirits. They would want to encourage them to move on and away from the body they have left behind, and from those who are still living.

Before the birth of physical bodies and three dimensions, we can imagine that biological decomposition was not an issue. A mortal life did not involve ageing, deteriorating, and rotting, but learning, maturing, and fading away. This theory defies the experience of physical death we have today but it is an interesting way to view prehistoric archaeology. Many of the very early burials start to make more sense when we look at them as anomalies, rather than new spiritual trends or symbols of status. It also explains why we are more likely to dig up 100 million-year-old dinosaur bones than 1 million-year-old human bones. The survival of these bones may not be down to avoiding the process of decomposition imposed by the laws of this dimension. How the bones got here would involve factors around what was happening to the person (or indeed the dinosaur). What made them collapse through to the penal colony instead of fading away back to their source when they died? After all, in a world where there is no time, what is 'a million years'?

Death of a natural death

Although these ideas are unusual from our modern perspective, when we consider them in context with the primitive psychology that we have studied so far, they do not seem so unreasonable. Brian Hayden, archaeologist and author of *A Prehistory of Religion: Shamans, Sorcerers and Saints,* reminds us of the conventional take on prehistoric religion:

> '…it appears that the mere act of intentionally burying a body during this time period [150,000 to 35,000 years ago] seems to indicate a special status for such individuals—minimally, an attempt to shield the body from the normal forces of disturbance, out of respect for that person and often probably in an attempt to create a more permanent location of burial that could be easily relocated and revisited.'

Considering what we now know about the primitive mind, we can say with confidence that a tribal hunter 150,000 years ago, or indeed 35,000 years ago, is unlikely to enact a ceremonial burial ritual 'out of respect' for the individual. This is not how primitive people behave; this is how *we* behave. Wailing, crying and then *forgetting* are respectful from a primitive perspective, as is *not* visiting the grave. These people, like the Neanderthals, related to everything around them. Their minds and bodies reflected their environment as their environment reflected them back again. True to an animistic lifeworld, there was no distinction between the two. Burials such as that of the Red Lady are representative of a profound social disturbance. Their world was changing. They did not understand what was happening to them and they did not know how to stop it. Perhaps they performed the ritual burials to send a message or an omen. The portals are breaking down. Death is not as it should be. We cannot get home.

By the time we reach settled farming communities 30,000 years later, solemn burial practices are more conceivable. This is because the principles with which people lived their lives had been altered. The nature of agriculture and domestication is such that the birth, growth, and death cycle is no longer a prescription for life in its true form. Neolithic farmers corrupted the natural cycle so that life and death are now engineered and controlled in a conscious way. But during the time of the Red Lady, those basic life principles still applied.

Mythical Gilgamesh is representative of these changes around life and death during the Neolithic period. He is so distraught when his wild brother dies that in his honour he throws off his royal robes and dons only a lion skin. He leaves his city and travels the lands. He is beside himself with grief, but a grief that seems to go beyond what is usual. He is frantic in his sorrow, fearful in his distress. He says over and over: 'I am afraid of death'. It is as if death is terrorizing him. He says, 'My friend whom I love has turned to clay', suggesting that the body of Enkidu is not as it should be. Could he be witnessing the birth of mortality as the delicate image of his wild friend solidifies before him? After he passes through the mountain portal, Gilgamesh meets with a wise man Ut-napishtim. Gilgamesh cries, 'The Snatchers have blocked my routes, Death is waiting in my bedroom and wherever I set my foot, Death is there too!' His words speak of profound changes to the process of dying. Who are the 'Snatchers', and why has this routine transformation become such an unbearable torture? Gilgamesh himself calls it a 'crisis'. He knows life on Earth is changing and that he is integral to those changes. He also knows that Enkidu, his dear friend, represented the last of wild strength and freedom. The grief and the guilt are too much to bear.

Does my bum look big in this?

So the burial of the Red Lady and others like him is not symbolic of some new Aurignacian trend. As well as the burial itself, the shells and ivory buried with him communicate anxiety and desperation. Adornment is another controversial subject we need to address, and one we will not be viewing as an evolutionary step towards the modern world of fashion. The use of items such as shells and animal bones within burials of this time-period coincides with the arrival of what experts call 'modern people'. Many writers of prehistory interpret this behaviour as representing the beginning of mankind's transition to consciousness and development of symbolic culture. They mark this transition with the archaeological finds of impressive art and jewellery. Apparently, we were learning how to think.

The simplicity and ritual life of the Cro-Magnon people, far from making them ignorant, made them impeccably competent survivors. We could say their skills and expertise in the practice of life on Earth were unsurpassable. Therefore, we need to find a catalyst that might explain these new behaviours, a jolt of such magnitude that *forces* them to start thinking outside the box, so to speak. From a primitive perspective, a 30,000-year-old nomadic hunter-gatherer would not wear seashells or bear's teeth to look attractive or to impress his neighbours. Immodesty and the assertion of personal power do not reflect the values that they demonstrate in the rest of their behaviour.

There are anthropologists who suggest that ancient people adorned themselves in order to communicate who they were to other tribes. However, clan identification is associated with territorial issues that accompany settlement and is rare in primitive nomads. It is not enough to say that nomadic humans suddenly developed a taste for vanity and power when they had been clever enough to avoid it for millions of years. Instead, if we consider the strong animism that was present in their lives, we can imagine that the one with all the bear's teeth around his neck is the one who is in *need* of the qualities that those teeth hold. Perhaps he is calling upon the bear's influence because of social pressures he has not experienced before.

The so-called Shaman's Grave in Israel is a burial of a 12,000-year-old Natufian woman. It is another interesting example of how people used animals to ward off strangeness. This particular grave is considerably later than those of the Aurignacian period but still has an interesting point to make. The Natufians were semi-sedentary hunter-gatherers in the Levant region of the Eastern Mediterranean, an area which includes Israel, Syria, and Jordan. Within the Natufian archaeology, we find extremely early signs of farming. The grave contained a woman who was pinned down by large stones. Numerous animal remains such as bear, eagle, wild boar, cow, and fifty tortoises accompanied her, as well as someone else's foot! For its time, this is very unusual behaviour. Experts have labelled her a shaman due to all the animal remains, but they do not address the uniqueness of the grave. When no one before had needed to perform this type of ritual burial, why did they need to do it with her? The fact that she does not appear to have been buried with a single tool of the shaman trade weakens her title of shaman. Instead, let us consider the reverse. Let us imagine that her tribe buried her with a rich adornment of animals, not because they revered her but because she scared them. Perhaps she was bringing bad luck to the clan or behaving in a ghostly or zombie-like way. This would explain the large stones that were pinning her down. The animal offerings would then have been to ward off *her* spirit in order to protect the tribe, to stop *her* from rising up and creating havoc. We know this period of time was difficult for tribes, mainly because changes were happening to people who were not supposed to be able to change. Hence, people employed the influence of animals to help with the difficulties that this transition brought.

We associate primitiveness with adornment because many native people today wear feathers, beads, teeth, and animal bones for a variety of reasons. But our ancient man did not wear these things. The Neanderthal people probably did not either. Animals and birds certainly do not. These items and practices demonstrate a move away from that pure primitiveness, which is such that an unconscious integral mind has no desire for them. Our prehistoric ancestors would have adorned themselves with objects to draw strength from the qualities of those objects because they were in need. If there are no objects, there is *no need*. I am of the view that it is not the case that humans developed an understanding of art and decoration for the sake of it, or because they were developing a particular kind of intelligence. The changes that were happening at the time drove our primitive ancestors to employ these magical items to help them cope. As the otherworld was collapsing, distorting, and even starting to disappear, people were clinging to it through these symbolic tokens. Perhaps they were attempting to please the spirits and keep them close, influence a change or for protection because they simply did not understand what was going on.

A cry for help

The extraordinary and perplexing European cave art associated with this time-period and the Cro-Magnon people also provides insights into this type of primitive mindset. We find many of the ancient cave paintings from the Upper Palaeolithic period in France and Spain. One of the most fascinating is the Chauvet-Pont-d'Arc Cave in the Ardèche region of southeast France where the paintings date to approximately 30,000 BCE. It is home to the oldest known cave art in the world.[5] When we talk about the Cro-Magnons as sophisticated modern humans,

---

[5] Except perhaps the famous hand prints at El Castillo in Northern Spain, which are possibly 40,000 years old.

we need to remember that at this time they upheld essentially primitive values. They did not farm, use complex language or have a distinct social hierarchy. They hunted, gathered, and fished; they lived in caves and used stone tools, albeit more refined when compared with their Neanderthal neighbours. So what were these primitive people doing painting in caves, in the dark, with a profound creative understanding of composition, perspective, and light? The contemporary nature and aesthetic quality of the paintings are as shocking as they are unexplainable. When we look at the rock art of tribes around today, we find charming stick-like line drawings and flat two-dimensional pictures. They depict stories with symbolic value and social relevance, but they also portray a simplicity and naivety we would expect from the primitive minds that have executed them. They do not inspire the type of religious experience that the Stone Age European art does. Even in medieval Europe many thousands of years on, art did not have the same quality of depth and sophistication as some of these cave paintings.

Many who have had the privilege of visiting these caves recall an overwhelming and often spiritual experience. On entering, some people are speechless. Others refer to the moment when they see the pictures for the first time as an 'emotional shock' or as if they are looking at 'a great masterpiece'. Many people liken this place to a Cro-Magnon cathedral where a spiritual atmosphere is tangible. Something momentous clearly took place here. I agree that these pictures, even in photographs, are very moving. So what is it about them that inspires such an emotional response? There are writers who say the artists were shamans who journeyed through the caves and tunnels. In trance-like states, they painted on the walls and ceilings in honour of the animals and the spirits they are depicting: human, horse, bison, rhino, lion. Most agree that these images of the hunter and the hunted are symbolic representations of their wild lifestyle. But what could be the catalyst for such dramatic artistic expression? We cannot assume to have another case of cultural evolution. The art and the extraordinary skill required for its delivery are too extreme to have developed, especially when there is nothing of its kind that precedes it. In fact, the more time passes, the less sophisticated the cave art becomes. What, then, was the trigger for this unprecedented artistry?

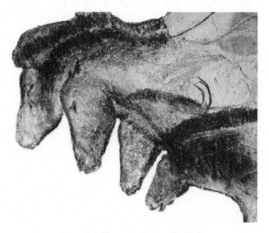

Horses from the Chauvet-Pont-d'Arc Cave

The pictures at Chauvet clearly have an emotional quality. They look like the expressions of people who are pouring their distress, frustration, and grief across the walls and ceilings of this cave. It is as if they are acting out a sort of Palaeolithic

Ghost Dance of their own. Art is well known as an expression of dysphoria. Strong and sometimes disturbing feelings run deep, overwhelming the individual and compelling them to create works of what we might call genius. The touching beauty of Van Gogh's sunflowers and the bewitching charm of his solitary chair were realized in this way. For many artists more recently, social and emotional turmoil is often the inspiration behind the creation of something astonishing and beautiful. These unique cave paintings look like this could be the case. They could be cries of a whole tribe, perhaps an entire species. It is as if the artists harnessed a vitality from within the cave and made it visible. They revealed a hidden natural force that we in the twenty-first century are able to witness through their art. Primitive minds should not have the capacity for imaginative statements like this if we believe that 'primitive mind' equals 'inferior brain'. But these minds could not have invoked the vitality we see here from within themselves because they had no within. It is a dynamism that primitive people are connected to which is abundant in nature and particularly strong within seams and portals such as caves. They knew this vitality well. Were the artists calling upon it to re-establish the link that would return them to their dimension of perception and the life they had been separated from?

Before this time, primitive people on Earth had no need for self-expression such as this dramatic art. They ritualized their sadness, joy, tragedy, and all the emotions that accompanied their simple lives, as if they were on a stage. They acted them out in a format and pattern they understood. To my eyes, these ground-breaking images do not represent a conscious desire to express thought. They are messages to people in the future. The Cro-Magnon people were immensely intelligent, emotional, talented, and original, but they were also troubled.

Stuck in time

This period of time marks a significant chapter in the story of humankind. To suggest that the Cro-Magnon people had become trapped here following their arrival from another dimension sounds like science fiction. But if we can imagine that portal technology existed in ancient times, it leaves us wondering what happened that put a stop to such a phenomenal process from working? How was linear time introduced to our perception? How did it wipe our memories of a timeless world? Why were these new humans trapped here? In fact, why are *we* trapped here now without the capacity to travel to parallel universes when we know in theory it is feasible to do so? Why do we only find cosmic tumbleweed blowing across the galaxies as we look out into the heavens for life forms that we might recognize?

By viewing the events of this period in this way we are creating a history for ourselves that is radically different to the one we know. These modern humans colonized Europe; they were the ancestors of what we would now term The West. In no time at all, the Neanderthal people had disappeared. We could say that the Cro-Magnons were the first colonists, but under considerable duress. They left behind them a tragic legacy considering the fate of indigenous people in the millennia that followed. Having said that, I do not believe that these people's descendants were responsible for introducing agriculture and settlement to the dimension of Earth. For this, we are dealing with another psychology altogether. It is a mind that does not have a primitive root, but a fear and loathing of anyone who does. At this point in time, another type of human appears on Earth: the Proprietor.

CHAPTER 9

Random Ancient Memories

'We know a lot about the conditions which create memories but
almost nothing about the causes of forgetting.'
Dr James L McGaugh[6]

ollowing on from the social disruption of the Upper
Palaeolithic, about 12,000 years ago as the last ice sheets
were melting across Europe, another phenomenon occurred: people started farming. From the remoteness of modernity, it is not easy to work out what inspired people to settle
down and start farming after living so long as nomadic hunters.
But as the revolution of all revolutions and the seam of all
seams, it stands out like a stone pyramid in the wilderness. It
also marks the end of the road for our egalitarian hunters.

Metamorphosis

Social activists such as environmental primitivists question the
benevolence of adopting an agricultural lifestyle. Our ancient

---

[6] Professor of Neurobiology at University of California, Irvine.

man would echo their point of view. I agree that it is difficult to argue in its favour when we consider what agriculture and complex society have led to: disease, poverty, war, overpopulation, environmental devastation, extreme inequality, social dependency, and divided communities. Nevertheless, it is the most significant lifestyle change in the *Homo* story so far, as it set us upon the road to civilization and to where we find ourselves today.

This era is particularly interesting to us as primitive psychologists because the transition to farming from hunting and gathering required a massive shift in human psychology. How did tribes who were unable to conceive of ideas outside their unconscious integrity, manage to hop outside that integrity and invent something that so radically opposed it? Contrary to what most textbooks tell us, agriculture was not an evolutionary forgone conclusion. We know that about 12,000 years ago nomadic hunter-gatherers were happily hunting and gathering. Although they were experiencing changes in the climate, wild food was *not* in short supply. Some prehistorians go so far as to refer to Mesolithic life as a Golden Age. There is no evidence of any specific conditions or events cataclysmic enough to trigger this extraordinary shift in lifestyle.

We also know that imposing farming and settlement on primitive cultures can ruin them. Many agricultural development programmes have failed in parts of Africa and Asia due to the social conflicts that the process of farming initiates: complexity, hierarchy, and ownership. It also involves a host of events that are not ritualized. The social dynamic of a primitive

clan is a simple but finely tuned affair. Ideas regarding the rank-
ing of status according to themes of planned 'work' rather than
intuitive 'roles' might not have been as easy as we think for ancient people to take on board. At the heart of this conflict is
ritual. Agriculture means we must adopt non-ritualized behaviour. In other words, instead of intuitive and repetitive daily
rituals, we act out a *learned sequence of events*. Hunter-gatherers
do not resist farming because it will lead to an unmanageable
population, pollution, and disease—as we know it does. They
resist it because it violates the ritualized and animistic framework of their community. This framework ensures they are immune to change according to primitive laws. We could say that
for primitive people, the act of hunting is a loophole ritual
warding off the shadow of domestication. Nomadism is a ritual
warding off the shadow of permanence. In general, tribal people do not regard civilized society as a successful recipe for daily
living. Natives do not see us as presenting a social template that
they can aspire to, but rather that a social disease has infected
our communities and is slowly destroying them.

There is evidence that the Neolithic tribes of Europe re-
sisted the introduction of farming and settlement. This new
way of life did not ripple steadily across the globe. Instead, we
see it taking hold in awkward fits and starts, and it also took a
substantial period of time.[7] In fact, resisting this transition
would have been instinctive, just as it is for primitive people
today.

---

[7] The most significant signs of Neolithic activity are found in the Fertile Cres-
cent and date to about 12,000 years ago, but agriculture didn't reach Britain
until roughly 6,000 years later.

The degradation of primitive principles that continues across parts of the world today reminds us of how new the development of civilization is in the context of the last few million years. The developing world appears to be stuck in a state in between primitive and civilized. It is in a perpetual *non*-state. The people who live in these broken communities look to the West, spellbound by her wealthy allure, but have become stranded between worlds. Deculturation has caused the terrible living conditions, civil war, starvation, and disease we witness in parts of Africa and Asia. Over many hundreds of years, invasion, colonial rule, and organized religion have defaced their wild tribal lives. Civilization, particularly farming, brought a new way of life: waged work, a restricted diet, mental and physical ill health, inequality, and conflict. Dominant civilized culture has reduced these once flourishing communities to situations involving the most desperate, physical survival. While these poor nations are busy providing the West with natural resources and cheap labour, thousands of people die of starvation, AIDS, and water borne diseases every day because they have abandoned their original way of life. Yet they are unable to civilize as effectively as we have in the West because they lack any political, financial or cultural autonomy. Wealthy nations continue to actively perpetuate their dependence through various means such as economics, religion, health and education, and the media. They are unable to break free from the dynamic that is responsible for their ruination in the first place.

The Middle East is another part of the world where modernization is proving to be an impossible transition. We see remnants of a tribal ethos resisting the influence of the United States and Europe. The cultural values and traditions in the Middle East clash with the Western principles of democracy and secularism with devastating results. This is perhaps a little ironic considering the principles of civilization first appeared in this region thousands of years ago. Perhaps the unrest we witness in the Middle East today is a reflection of the original 10,000-year-old conflict, an echo of past attempts to resist an overpowering intrusion. Only in the West have we been able to establish civilized principles and refine them to such a degree that no trace of a tribal mindset remains to conflict with them.

We will be viewing the metamorphosis from hunting to farming, from primitive to civilized, in terms of two dimensions colliding. This is in line with a layered, as opposed to a linear, idea of reality. We will not be looking at it as an inevitable stage in human development. We now know a little about one of these dimensions—the primeval dimension—which we could also call the 'indigenous dimension'. But what of the world it collided with?

Whatever it was and wherever it came from, it attacked the immunity that had protected primitive people from change for many thousands of years. It worked by breaking down the natural resistance to progress that is inherent in all living things, making mankind vulnerable to the extremes that followed. Immediately this collision occurred, the gates opened. Like a dam bursting, torrents of alien newness rushed in and engulfed our species. In less than 5,000 years, subtlety and timelessness gave way to the physical weight and containment of three dimensions. Buildings and temples like the pyramids and ziggurats start to appear. We travelled from egalitarian harmony to dominance and servitude in even less time. As these two worlds met head-on, new principles of life rained down upon the world. Modern history replaced ancient memory in what seems like the blink of an eye.

I must remember. . .

Our memories are like maps. Professor Jeremy Brotton, author of *A History of the World in Twelve Maps,* says that we can only have a true picture of the environment at a ratio of 1:1. At any other scale, we have to make decisions about what to include and what to leave out. Maps are therefore subjective reflections of the map-maker. We cannot have an impartial image of the world that is not life size. Jorge Luis Borges explores this principle in his short story *On Exactitude in Science.* In the story, an Empire creates an imperial map so detailed that it ends up the size of the Empire itself. And so it is the case with history and also our personal memories. Maps, memories, and history share the same problem of scale and recollection because they are always second-hand. They are never original, always derived. A memory at the ratio of 1:1 becomes the experience, just like Borges' map. This then suggests that we also edit our memories because we do not act them out each time we recall them. Like the map-maker, we too must make decisions about what to include and what to leave out from the original experience.

The slightly unsettling part of this scenario is that we are not conscious of how our minds make the selection. We are not aware of editing our memories during the retrieval process: we simply remember. This lack of awareness means that our memories are vulnerable to interference and influence. How do we know that what we are retrieving is accurate and true? Tampering of any kind would render them unreliable. We could find ourselves remembering things that never happened at all. A psychological study carried out at the University of Hull in 2010 supports this idea. Researchers were studying the nature of memory and reported that twenty per cent of people vividly recalled incidents that never took place. The fact that these people believe they *did* take place illustrates that we have no awareness of how the retrieval process works. This discrepancy makes it possible for something other than ourselves to be in control of what we *think* we remember, how we remember it, and when. From the perspective of a computer simulation, a program could create, recreate or update our memories every time we go to retrieve one. We would accept it as a reliable copy of something that really happened, none the wiser. Stories such as Total Recall and The Matrix explore this idea in fantastical terms, but the sort of control we are talking about is not fictional. It is real, influential, and primitive at its heart.

What our million-year-old man might refer to as 'shadow influence' can have a significant effect on what we believe to be true about events, conversations or any moment that has passed in our lifetime.[8] Modern psychologists call it *cognitive distortion*. Cognitive distortions are thoughts that cause us to perceive a defective version of reality. Influences can affect us, or rather

---

[8] In primitive terms, shadow influence is not 'bad' because there is no moral good and bad. It is more constructive to see it as 'negative' and therefore potentially destructive.

infect us, seemingly without us knowing, transforming how we remember and interpret events. A memory may be twisted out of shape once we have processed and retrieved it via our personal inner worlds. There, unsupervised by the rest of the community, it can take on a life of its own and become disfigured. This potential loophole in our psychological profile serves to weaken our relationships with one another because it impacts on the way we communicate. It is the back door through which shadows, or negative psychological influences, can sneak in. They make themselves at home and start twiddling knobs without anyone even noticing. When this happens it manifests in the form of distorted thinking. Our past experiences affect the decisions we make now. These shadow influences bend the past out of shape which then undermines our ability to make sound judgements about the present based on the facts of the moment. The process creates a vicious circle in which we can become vulnerable to further psychological influence. To make matters worse, we do not confront our distorted thinking patterns because the controlling influences lead us to believe that there is in fact nothing wrong. We are adamant that our assessment of the situation is an accurate one. We finally arrive in a state of denial and living with a false perception of reality which we believe to be perfectly normal. In Borges' story, when the Empire crumbles, all that remains is the map.

So, how do we know that in terms of memory we are drawing off something authentic and not something that is simulated, distorted or implanted? What if our misshapen memories are contributing to a distorted perception of our 'now' reality? The truth is, we are simply unable to answer these questions.

There is no measure of control we can put in place to cater for this defect, even though our relationships and lifestyles rely heavily on memory to function.

Instinct and intuition work very differently. These primitive tools do not recycle potentially corrupt information from our past experience. They draw from an original and natural source—a template—which we would once have had access to. Our senses, coupled with this source, would have steered us through our lives, assisted by the knowledge of elders in the tribe and omens in the environment. Memory has replaced these instincts, just as history has replaced myth, and biology animism. We have created a string of physical events out of a centred and timeless origin. This new way of perceiving everything as a sequence rather than a whole framework was in part responsible for breaking down our immunity to change during the Neolithic Revolution. Consequently, we have become anxious about the future and subject to a deluge of influence that we cannot control. Our psychological complexity, while elevating us above the rest of the nature, exposes our personal worlds to all sorts of psychological threats and coercion that we struggle to resist. And we no longer have a reliable template with which to gauge all the information we receive. Our social laws have become vague, our moral codes littered with contradictions. This hidden chaos contributes to many of the psychiatric illnesses and personality disorders civilized people suffer from today. It appears that the ability to develop has come at a hefty price.

Primitive minds do not depend on memory. They are able to maintain this independence because of the lack of linear processes present in their daily life. The cycles of ritual and routine that they act out do not require the conscious recollection of sequences in a certain arrangement. A wonderful example of this is in Daniel Everett's book, where he describes the Pirahãs learning how to make Brazilian canoes.

The Brazilian canoes were superior to the Pirahãs' primitive canoes and much sought after by them. Everett had the idea that they could learn how to make their own, so he traded some tools and arranged for a canoe builder to visit the camp to show them how to do it. The tribe spent the day happily making their Brazilian canoe, but once the builder had gone never did it again. They stated categorically 'Pirahãs don't build canoes!' This behaviour demonstrates their inability to retain the sequence of events that would enable them to build the canoe. It is outside their usual ritual and routine. It is 'foreign knowledge' (Everett) that requires the use of memory instead of instinct to function. To us, this might seem stupid, but it is *immunity to progress* superbly executed. It is also the foundation for strong social relationships. By not retaining foreign knowledge in this way, the Pirahãs do not make themselves vulnerable to the potential consequences of unreliable or infected memories. By continuing to build their own, albeit inferior canoes, they are covering a loophole. It prevents shadows that prey on the sequence of memory from destabilising their view of the world and each other.

For a primitive clan whose instincts are intact and whose ritual life is flourishing, how and why would they give it all up and start farming? In fact, the more we talk about the remarkable law and order that underpins the primitive psychology, the more impossible it seems. We know that small-scale farming is acceptable for some small and remote tribes if the activities do not clash with the basic principles of their primitive lifestyle. But, we also know that large-scale farming, domestication, and settlement can be devastating for primitive hunter-gatherer communities. We can assume that it was also the case 10,000 or so years ago. The psychological disparities would have applied in the same way.

Agriculture and all that accompanies it is the single biggest factor contributing to our removal from the timeless past. Planting makes us mindful of where and when to sow seeds, how long they take to grow, and when to harvest the crop. We have to plan for the future and work at specific times of the day, month, and year. These activities are immensely difficult for primitive tribal people to keep up for any length of time. Farming engineers a new version of the birth, growth, and death cycle, one that exists outside of what is natural and instinctive. It stretches the cycle to resemble the linear set-up we are now familiar with. If a crop fails, we have a past that contains hard work and failure, and a future that contains hunger and anxiety. Forward planning replaces spontaneity, project management instinct.

Nowadays, undisturbed hunter-gatherers are almost non-existent, so it is an interesting exercise to imagine a world where the farming communities are the minority as they would have been in the early Neolithic period. Like the European invaders of America and Australia in more recent times, the Neolithic farmers in Europe would have met with naive and innocent indigenous communities. Like the Pirahãs and their canoes, it is difficult to imagine how Neolithic hunters could invent or adopt this new way of life without radical intervention of some kind.

Attack of the clones

Why did primitive people stop hunting and start farming? There are two scenarios we are going to talk about that will help us to answer this question. First, during the two-world collision, a new species of *Homo* 'appeared' that managed life in a conscious and ordered way. Second, these new people brainwashed the indigenous tribes into breaking their contract with the primitive laws, enslaving them through the medium of a kind of sorcery.

Considering the conflict in psychology at this time, which we have discussed at length, we can assume to have at least two different types of person on Earth during the late Mesolithic period. One can civilize, the other is immune to civilization or at least resists it. One works with the arrow of time and the other blends with natural cycles. One knows how to manage nature and the other is integral to nature. From this description, these people do not appear to belong to the same species. But our genus classification system, based on the Darwinian principle of common descent, states that *Homo sapiens* (wise man) was the only distinct species on Earth at the time agriculture was getting under way. From the point of view of human psychology, this classification system is deficient.

If we focus on the psychology rather than the biology of these humans, it is as if the agrarian revolutionaries had beamed down from another planet. They possessed a unique mindset distinct from the Palaeolithic hunters. They interpreted, managed, and organized life in a completely different way. The Cro-Magnon people and their descendants, although sophisticated in primitive terms, observed essentially primitive values. They were great warriors, artists, and hunters, but not farmers, administrators or hoarders.

These strange new people we will call the Proprietors. I am using this word to make a point. Although their bones appear to be physiologically similar to the tribal people of the era, they clearly had an immense capacity for conscious thought control that made them flagrantly different. This mindset enabled new systematic modes of behaviour that were almost mechanical in comparison. Land clearance, planting, irrigation, temple building, town planning, and political hierarchy all require a magnitude of organization and administration, none of which primitive hunters could have managed. This is not because they are lazy or stupid, but because these tasks have no ritualistic foundation. As we have discussed, primitive ritual is repetitive behaviour that ensures your species does not change (see Chapter 2). Any new rituals that people introduced to assist the farming process, such as to make the sun shine or the rain fall so that crops would grow were ceremonial, not habitual. A desert nomad who sings to the sky when rain has not fallen for months is distinct from a farmer asking the gods for rain to water his crops and herds. As the former, you are a part of the landscape. As the latter, the landscape is a part of you. This is a subtle difference, but in terms of how primitive people perceive and relate to their environment, it is significant.

Within the ancient cuneiform and proto-cuneiform texts of Persia and Mesopotamia[9] are where these administrative activities really come to light. Agriculture in the ancient Middle East 10,000 years ago consisted of quaint small-scale subsistence activities. But it did not take long for it to become a military-style operation on a vast scale, which also led to the formation of state societies and political hierarchies. The Proprietors invented writing here around 5,000 years ago. They developed it initially for administrative purposes; the writing down of myths, stories, and poetry followed later. The level of bureaucracy that the writing enabled is breathtaking: detailed accounts, inventories, payment distribution, and personnel records. These are all organizational tools we recognize in a modern business today. In fact, Mesopotamia was using numbering systems involving counters and pictographs for about 1,000 years before writing even began.

The social and economic organization that grew in the villages and towns of Mesopotamia bears a remarkable resemblance to the structure we have today. A tributary economy is one of the earliest forms of economic management from that region. Individual households produced wares such as cloth, pottery, and food that they 'donated' to a central administration for distribution. Any surplus was committed to the treasury. This form of social governance introduces an extremely non-

---

[9] Modern day Afghanistan and Iraq.

primitive way of organizing society. We know that the imposed hierarchy and lack of equality and autonomy are at odds with primitive tribal life. But perhaps more relevant is that a primitive mind would not have been able to undertake these heavily administrative tasks. We tend to think that bureaucracy emerges slowly as a system evolves. As management tools, administrative procedures unfold in line with the growing intricacies of our affairs. But, complexity like this can only develop if a psychology exists that is able to cope with the bureaucracy in the first place. Remember, in eight months the Pirahãs could not even learn to count to ten. We also think that this level of sophistication did not arrive until much later on in the Bronze Age or even the Iron Age. In fact, 4,000 years before Greece and Rome hit the big time, it was all going on in the Middle East.[10] This ancient regime is our first recording of social inequality and civil service on a significant scale. The people who devised and executed this new regulatory lifestyle were never primitive hunters. They were clued-up and experienced in the mechanics of civilization.

Anyone running a business with employees today will be familiar with the predicament of managing people and their activities. It is a difficult affair within any organization to instruct, guide, and motivate the workforce. Even today, people are still innately resistant to change and quick to resent inequality if it is crudely handled. This makes managing and motivating individuals within a hierarchy a delicate and complex craft. So how

---

[10] China's Neolithic period also started early, but for the purposes of this book our main focus is the Middle East and Europe.

exactly did these ancient administrators get tribal people who could not work like this to work like this?

Methods of thought reform

This question leads us to our second transition theory—brainwashing. What psychologists today refer to as *coercive persuasion* was an unmistakeable part of life 10,000 years ago and doubtless much earlier. More appropriate terms in relation to a primitive mind would be 'mesmerism' or 'enchantment'.

Over time, modern people have learned to accept the socioeconomic structure of their lives. Mesolithic people had not. As far as they were concerned, the practice of civilizing was presenting a peculiar set of principles that they were never going to embrace. How, then, did the new Proprietors design and initiate a conditioning process that was so successful? The archaeology tells us that it was not entirely down to brute force. The idea of enticing them with food and shelter does not work either. In any society, nomadism and the freedom to hunt and gather food only become problematic when individual property rights have taken over the wild and communal ground. Primitive people would not have initiated this move to farming because of a need to survive. Their ability to survive and their harmonious lives were not in need of an overhaul. In fact, Mesolithic life could not have been better. Instead, we have elite groups clearly wanting control over people and land. Agriculture was the way they instigated it. Primitive tribal people, even as sophisticated as the Cro-Magnons, simply would not have accepted this situation. Unless they were put under a spell.

Enchantment is an age-old practice. At its heart is a language that involves animism, influence, and intention, so ancient primitive people would have spoken it fluently. In ancient stories, mesmerizing and spellbinding are commonplace and suited to the immaterial nature of a timeless and mythical realm. There were once otherworldly spirits who made it their business to test your psychological endurance. Water nymphs enchanted young men to their delirious deaths. To look upon the Gorgon Medusa would turn you to stone. Even the woodland queen Titania becomes besotted with an ass. We usually find the lesson within these stories is the same: be vigilant and alert when stepping outside the door, or through a portal. We witness this cautious attitude in the rituals and behaviour of tribal people who are still around today. Complacency is dangerous.

Here is a vital key to our investigation: enchantment is an otherworldly business. This is why civilized cultures make such light of its effects. Coercive persuasion, operant conditioning, subliminal stimuli, hypnotic induction—these are aspects of mind control that we are victims of in Western society. Yet, based on invisible forces of mental trickery and sorcery, their roots lie in a primitive otherworld. They are all ancient practices.

Many tribespeople associate trickery and sorcery with a lower or under world. A Pirahã child caught malaria because she stepped on a leaf which her family believed contained a spell from a lowerworldly spirit. All through time and across the world there are stories just like this, tales of gods and spirits casting spells and inflicting sickness. The preventative medicine is always the same: be mindful of those spirits and their influence, do not entertain them or aggravate them, and always stick to the rituals.

For this reason, primitive people are humble in the presence of the otherworld. As far as they are concerned, we are always in the presence of the otherworld. The effects that these influences wield in tribal life are the same effects that we in the modern world choose to ignore at our peril. The primitive rituals acknowledge and respect these influences and thereby keep enchantments at bay. Strong fevers deliver us into realms of sensation and imagery within which our resilience to shadows and illusion is tested. It is only in the last three hundred years or so that scientists began to discredit the belief that illness is the influence of a 'spirit' or 'energy' that they cannot explain. But even with the phenomenal advancements of recent years, so much remains unexplained by scientists and doctors. They can name factors within our lifestyle or genetic make-up that are likely contributors to diseases like cancer or Alzheimer's, but they cannot name the exact cause in individual cases. While diagnosis and treatment have improved, identifying the reason *why* it has developed in a particular person is still impossible. As we discussed in Chapter 7, rarely is an individual's psychology considered to be part of the problem.

The power of *Vimna*

In the beginning, the cultivation of crops would not have been just a physical practice. During this time, the primitive otherworld was still alive in people's perception, so planting would have involved this psychology. Therefore, the first farmers would have called upon an enterprise that was prevalent in everyone's lives at that time: the vitality within nature.

As I am constantly referring to this invisible force that nature wields, I am going to give it a name—*vimna*. This is taken from the word *vim* meaning 'strength, force, power, energy'. It is also a play with the Sanskrit word *vimana*, which literally translated means 'measuring out, traversing' or 'having been measured out'—a befitting reference to the three-dimensional collapse. We need to view *vimna* in the traditional way, as a fundamental, primeval force in nature that has an intention independent of the human mind.

The cave artists harnessed *vimna*. It is the current that carries us through a transformation. It is the power that drives a meteor shower. It designs the clouds, makes the rain fall, and persuades a tiny seed to grow. So far, science has been unable to find the source of this energy or vitality, and mathematicians cannot find an equation for it. In actual fact, scientists usually scoff at the mere mention of such a thing. We experience it, however, in the precision of seagulls wheeling in the sky, and in the ceaseless flow of a waterfall. It is the catalyst for seasons to change; it is what gets a bumblebee off the ground. When inspired humans create something awesome, there we see it too. William Shakespeare knew *vimna* well, as did many great writers, artists, and scientists throughout history, such as Einstein, Mozart, and Van Gogh. It is not their humanness that makes the work of these people great, but their ability to tap into a creative force that is timeless and species-less. A seagull may not be able to read a Shakespeare play, but the bird and the playwright share the ability to harness that which is above and beyond what they are as molecules to create something truly breathtaking. Primeval nature in the form of *vimna* can embrace our activities when we demonstrate values that it recognizes in them. Whether we are primitive or not, this must be the upside of having an artificial dimension woven into a natural platform. Some call it divine intervention; others call it genius.

In ancient Rome, a genius was a tutelary or guiding spirit. This spirit occupied all things, not just humans but animals and objects too. The Roman people believed that the genius part of the soul enabled and guided the production of wonderful creations. The word also has an Indo-European root *gen* meaning 'produce', which connects to the *gen*ie of the lamp who was also a tutelary spirit. This suggests that we once held the values derived from the *djinn* initiations in high esteem.

Watching a Shakespeare play is like watching seagulls wheeling, stars falling or a full moon silently rising. These are moments filled with *vimna*. They stimulate our emotions and touch an invisible part of us, but they are not spiritual. Seagulls are not spiritual beings, nor is our ancient axeman. He is initiated, challenged, able to give up that which he does not need, and capable of transformation and blending with his tribe. His emotionality merely ensures he never falters from where nature's laws say he should be. His emotions are not dramatic, intense or complicated because he does not live in a world of cutting extremes and contradictions. He has not developed consciousness or thought control, through which his emotions and behaviour are managed. Instead, he lives lightly within the space between the seagulls as they glide and Shakespeare's words as they fall from the page or from our lips. Within this space is an entire universe, timeless and discrete. Our lost, forbidden dimension resides here. From this place, the rigid passage of time looks small and dense indeed. But when *vimna* pierces through, miracles happen.

The enchantment of nature

The Nyae Nyae !Kung Bushmen also have a word for this natural, invisible force: n/um,[11] which Lorna Marshall describes:

> 'There is n/um in the sun, in falling stars, and in rain. A fire that has been specially kindled with fire sticks for ritual purposes has n/um. Ostrich eggs, bees, and honey have very strong n/um. Blood and milk have n/um. The n/umsi of menstrual blood and women's milk are especially strong. Elands and Giraffes have exceedingly strong n/um.'

Marshall goes on to describe how the n/um of different things has specific effects and uses, such as for protection, healing the sick and even inducing madness. The Bushmen refer to the n/um as 'strong'; it even holds the power of life and death. They say that the n/um of the gods is so strong it gives them extraordinary powers that no human could ever possess. They believe that their ancestors had far greater powers of n/um than anyone would have today.

---

[11] The symbol / denotes a click sound, one of four lingual clicks that the !Kung use. This one is called a dental click. 'The tip of the tongue is placed against the back of the upper front teeth; in the release, it is pulled away with a fricative sound' (Marshall)—it is a similar sound to our disapproving 'tut'.

When the Bushmen go into trance during their healing rituals, the healers see spirits lurking in the shadows—the deathbringers—and chase them off. They 'scold the gods'. These men are mentally strong enough to handle mesmerism under the controlled conditions of the ritual. The tribe treasures these men as they perform the ritual on everyone's behalf. They say that the healers have strong n/um and this is what enables them to go into trance. It also stops them from becoming overwhelmed while they interact with the spirits. The Bushmen are also wary of speaking the names of certain gods. They might attract their unwanted attention and put a spell on them, which could make them sick.

The word *trance* comes from Old French *transe*, 'fear of coming evil', but it originally meant 'passage from life to death' or 'cross-over'. *En,* meaning 'to put in', tells us *en-trance* is the act of engineering that passage from life to death, or from one place to another. It also represents a portal or doorway. The roots of these words show us how the art of transformation has become something we now fear. They also support the idea that enchantment is an otherworldly influence. To become entranced is to travel a seam inhabited by strong influences. It is an alien environment where we are vulnerable to spells, bad luck, and even death. The !Kung healers are great managers of these seams because they go into them on purpose without fear to protect their people from sickness. This principle is the same for other indigenous medicine people who manage the practice of otherworldly communication on behalf of their tribe. In civilized society, an *entrance* is one way through a physical door. It is no longer something to be wary of within the twilight or the dawn, or when there is a sudden change in the weather. Complacency has overwhelmed us.

When the dimensional collision took place and the Proprietors appeared on the scene, a powerful personality arrived with them: the sorcerer, 'one who influences'. The word *magician* comes from Old Persian *magush* meaning 'to be able to have power'. It later came to mean 'learned and priestly class', as in the biblical three wise men, the *Magi*. Here we are identifying a new authority that we need to be aware of. Nowadays, we find sorcerers and magicians in children's fairy stories, but in ancient times they were individuals within a community who wielded an impressive psychological power. This is a power that was normally held exclusively by the otherworldly spirits. To primitive people, it would have made him or her unduly intimidating and menacing. I must point out here that sorcerers are not the same as tribal shamans or medicine people. Many people view them as synonymous due to their 'magical' position, but there is a significant difference between them which we need to understand. Sorcerers wield influence. They use otherworldly means to mesmerize people and by doing so break the primitive law that says if you are powerful you must demonstrate *more* humility than anyone else. Otherwise, you are dangerous. On the other hand, the role of a primitive shaman is to protect their tribe from the destructive influences of the *natural spirits* who legitimately wield this power. Like the !Kung healers, they manage the otherworldly affairs on behalf of their people.

The *djinn* are examples of legitimate spirits in this regard. In the Middle East, there are communities and tribes that still fear them. They once occupied powerful places such as vast, ancient caves where *vimna* was strong and where they taught humans essential lessons about life. If we did not learn these lessons, we would reap the inevitable consequences. Sorcerers, however, were a new breed of being. They assumed the same powers but brandished them in devious ways for their own ends. For this reason, the Proprietors employed these sorcerers to manage a specific job for them on Earth: the conditioning department.

God forbid

During the two-world collision where we meet civilized principles for the first time, the pantheon of Sumerian[12] gods also arrived in Mesopotamia.

They descended from the heavens, set up camp on Earth, and implemented some revolutionary political and religious reforms. They introduced a new dynamic of ruler and subject into the otherworldly affairs between people and spirits that had not existed before. We usually view the myths in which we find these gods as simple, regional folktales. We imagine they tell stories of mankind's humble beginnings and that they were composed long after the events had taken place. But this book challenges the idea that civilization has evolved. I am suggesting that these changes were imposed. Therefore, we will be viewing these gods as the catalysts of devastating change and not as retrospective symbols of a developing human ideology. The

---

[12] Sumerians were a non-semitic people who occupied southern Mesopotamia from around 5000 BCE.

themes of these stories relate to the ethos of the administrative Proprietors, their workers, and the political changes happening at this time. These gods or influences were patriarchal, controlling, and businesslike. These are not traits we find in the more sensual and androgynous animistic spirits belonging to nature. A relationship with the environment, such as with rocks and trees, mountains and sky, keeps primitive people integral to their dimension of reality and ticking along as they need to. These new gods did not uphold such an exchange. Instead, they presented a new dynamic that involved threatening death and disaster to anyone who did not comply with their new rules.

Anu is the great Sumerian sky god and lord of all the gods. He is the father of Enki and Enlil. Enki is the teacher of civilization to mankind. His brother Enlil is king of all the populated lands. Anu sends his two sons to Earth to set up command posts. They bring with them gods such as Ennugi the canal-controller and Ninurta their chamberlain, who assist with their organization. They are orderly and efficient in dealing with their affairs. They bear no resemblance to the wild nature spirits that belonged to the primitives. The brothers employ some younger sky gods known as the Igigi to carry out the physical work on Earth. The Igigi tire of toiling the land and complain to Enlil about their lot. In the ancient Sumerian tale of *Atrahasis*[13] from the early second millennium BCE, the Igigi protest:

"'Every single one of us gods
Declared war.

---

[13] Atrahasis is a wise man and as precursor to Noah is a prominent figure in this region from an early period.

We have put [a stop] to the digging.
The load is excessive, it is killing us,
Our work is too hard, the trouble too much.'" (Dalley 2008)

The story of *Atrahasis* is a creation myth. It seems that whatever the gods were up to on Earth (which is unclear, but it appears to have involved a lot of digging), the Igigi became disgruntled. Enlil, along with his father Anu, upheld their complaints. They ordered the creation of mankind as slaves to do the work for them. They set about making humans out of clay and the blood of a sacrificed god Llawela. Enki could not contain his excitement:

"'Nintu [mistress of the gods] shall mix clay
With his flesh and his blood.
Then a god and a man
Will be mixed together in clay.
Let us hear the drumbeat forever after,
Let a ghost come into existence from the god's flesh,
Let her proclaim it as his living sign,
And let the ghost exist so as not to forget.'"

This account of human creation is grisly to say the least, yet it is one of the earliest we have. It is a bleak portrait of how civilized man was born in a laboratory for one purpose only: slavery. We can view this story as a creation myth—a cultural reflection of our origins—or as a true account of what happened at the time, but either way, it is not a pleasant rendering of mankind's birth. The haunting words tell of how the gods mixed nature's earth with an otherworldly influence to make a ghost. These ghosts are our civilized administrators and technicians of innovation and progress. They are the Proprietors. *They* are our ancestors.

The gods of birth and fertility in Sumer were also gods of forging, mining, and smelting. There are gods in other pantheons too, such as in ancient Greece, where fertility and forging are synonymous. This is because they exhibit the same propensity for engineering a creation from a set of ingredients. Hephaestus in the Greek pantheon is the god of blacksmiths and forging. He is also called upon by Zeus to create Pandora who he sends to Earth to curse mankind. (This is something we find Enlil doing later on in the story of *Atrahasis*.) On a more earthly note, we find prehistoric sorcerers buried with metal-working or forging tools for the same reasons. The Bronze Age 'Shaman' Grave located near Stonehenge is the grave of what was once a powerful sorcerer. He presents a commanding image buried in his cloak edged with thirty-six bone points and adorned with boar's tusks. He is also buried with the tools of a goldsmith placed at his feet.

In many mythical stories, we find the gods behaving like an elite political group, dictating creation, life, and death way beyond what primitive tribal people would understand. It reflects a dynamic that we live with today, except that today our gods are scientists. In the story of *Atrahasis,* we appear to have an embryonic research laboratory in which beings are meddling with the fundamentals of life. They are forging and inventing, pioneering even, but also destroying what is original in order to fuel their own agenda. Their behaviour does not relate to the original principles of this primitive world.

The content of these myths shows us a world of artificiality and discrimination being born, a world we unfortunately recognize. The emotive lines of poetry make clear the separation of man from his natural integrity as the gods govern over human mortality and our new-found civilization. They tell us to work hard. They tell us that nature does not love or care for us; we should fear the wild and subdue it. There is only one god who truly has our interests at heart—Enki. This solitary friend of man is echoed in the many saviours and prophets we meet in the religious stories that followed him.

One thing the Sumerian gods did not do when they created man was provide him with a lifespan. This is an interesting point that connects the administrative Sumerians to the primeval dimension. Having no lifespan speaks of immortality and non-linearity, a time before Time was invented, before a corpse was created. However, the new humans reproduced so profusely that the gods had to invent mortality in an attempt to limit their numbers: '[the gods] did not mark out the days for death but they did so for life' (*The Epic of Gilgamesh*). But as we know only too well, their plan did not work. Mortality has not prevented mankind from multiplying; it has only created an obsession with *not* dying. Civilization, modern man, and linear time were the ingredients for the creation of 'a generation'.

Unfortunately for mankind, introducing mortality was not enough to curb its proliferation, and its presence on Earth started to thoroughly aggravate Enlil. His brother's beloved clay people grew in such numbers and noise that Enlil's disgust turned to rage:

"'Cut off food supplies to the people!
Let the vegetation be too scant for their hunger!
Let Adad wipe away his rain.
Below let no flood-water flow from the springs.
Let wind go, let it strip the ground bear,
Let clouds gather but not drop the rain,
Let the field yield a diminished harvest,
Let Nissaba [goddess of cultivation] stop up her bosom.
No happiness shall come to them.'"

These gods are sorcerers. They wield an authority that is not naturally theirs to wield. They dictate and terrorize without giving mankind an opportunity to learn through ritual how to behave. Ritual, initiation, and transformation perpetuate life within the original template on Earth. But this scenario presents a different dynamic, one that our ancient man would not recognize.

Enlil's curse on mankind is merciless. It is chilling how each line grimly describes the problems we face in the world today. As these gods or sorcerers existed in a time when there was no time, then this curse would not know time either. It exists perpetually in the here and now, repeating itself to us over and over again like a ceaseless echo—"No happiness shall come to them'". And from mankind there is no response. We do not deny or contest these words because it is *only a story*, just like that of the Minotaur. It is an influence that these sorcerers configured outside the passage of time, so we grow more submissive and unresponsive as time goes by. We have fallen asleep, mesmerized by a spell that was cast thousands of years ago.

CHAPTER 10

Monumental Collapse

'It will take a miracle to free the human mind: because the chains are
magical in the first place.'
Norman O Brown

The appearance of outlandish new people and their revolutionary complex society was a lot for primitive
clans to cope with during the Neolithic period. But accompanying these changes was yet another bizarre phenomenon that they had imposed upon them: monumental stone
architecture. About 5,000 or so years ago, impossible feats of
engineering started popping up across the world—pyramids,
stone circles, dolmen, and burial tombs. Archaeologists have
long associated these edifices with what is turning out to be a
principal subject of this book: death. Experts also tell us that
they were built in accordance with our physical three-dimensional laws, by people who lived in huts, used stone tools, and
who had no understanding of metrology or measurement.

In the first instance, these staggering constructions disrupt
the developmental nature of engineering as we understand it

today. Chronologically, we would expect to find smaller buildings or temples that in turn lead to slightly bigger and better ones as the technology is refined over time. In other words, we might expect to find a small stone house on Salisbury Plain in Wiltshire before an intimidating construction like Stonehenge appears. As it is, the technical evolution of the construction of temples and dwellings over time demonstrates no connection to these megalithic structures. Even in Iron Age Britain 3,000 years later, people are still living in huts made of mud. This means that the Neolithic monuments had no impact on the development of construction at all. Man-the-builder goes from mud hut to pyramid, from clay hut to Stonehenge, with nothing in between. Like the Cro-Magnon people and their cave paintings, we cannot find the incremental steps that led to the phenomenon, which strongly suggests that these buildings were not about feats of engineering at all. They rise up out of the landscape like ghostly apparitions and unreservedly defy the classical laws of mass and inertia that belong to this dimension. But if primitive people were able to carry huge stones hundreds of miles and position them in impossible arrangements for the sake of religion, it is perplexing as to why they did not use those skills to build anything else.

A remarkable example of this type of construction is that of Gobekli Tepe in south-eastern Turkey. This stone monument dates back as far as 12,000 years making it the oldest of its kind in the world. It consists of about two hundred large T-shaped upright pillars that are arranged in circular formations and decorated with carved reliefs of a variety of animals and insects. What makes this monument particularly interesting is that it was built in a region and at a time where there are no signs of the transition to farming and settlement. It preceded social complexity. Experts claim it to be the oldest religious temple in the world, although it is not aligned with the stars or a celestial event such as solstice or equinox as far as we can make out. Archaeologists are vague about *why* people suddenly felt the need to create such a strange edifice, but they describe it as religious nonetheless.

From a multidimensional perspective, this stone monument materializes in our physical world like a mirage in the desert. Its mysterious, supernatural nature implies that it is, in essence, an *otherworldly* creation as opposed to a *religious* edifice built in three-dimensional space. At this point, it is important to make clear the distinction between otherworldly and religious. From an otherworldly perspective, the monument has been engineered according to the natural laws of integrity that relate to primitive animism and spirit activity. From a religious perspective, it is the product of a dualistic ideology belonging to a conscious mind. The latter, therefore, attaches it to modern ideas and not primitive principles.

From the perspective of a primitive psychology, the Gobekli Tepe temple does not work as part of an ideology. The bizarre image that emerges out of nowhere for no obvious reason is incongruous with the social context we find it existing within. If those who built the monument had not the capacity for agriculture, then the construction of a religious building as a statement of a new faith or as a place of worship does not fit their psychological profile. Hence, we cannot comfortably claim that primitive hunter-gatherers had anything to do with its construction.

Another remarkable point regarding Gobekli Tepe is that about a thousand years or so after it materialized, it appears to have been just as mysteriously covered up. Each part of the site was intentionally buried and made to look like it had never existed. There are two possible scenarios that might explain this. Perhaps those who had built it became frightened of what it was attracting in terms of bad luck or strange omens. Or, tribal rebels may have filled it in as a protest against the use of otherworldly technology in this way. Either way, we now know enough about the primitive mind to be confident that it was not indigenous tribespeople who were the creators of this extraordinary structure. It was not that they lacked the technology or the engineering know-how. It was that they would not have understood the *intention* required to construct it.

Precision engineering

When the two worlds met head-on during this time in the late Stone Age, the orderly and domineering collided with the primeval and animistic. It sent shock waves reverberating around the globe. The megalithic monuments dramatically depict this clash of worlds. They are symbolic of the fusion between two fiercely contrasting sets of principles that came together for the first time.

Ancient alien theorists suggest that the geometrical principles with which people designed Stonehenge, the Egyptian pyramids, and other monuments, originated on another planet or in another dimension. They believe that they somehow landed on the doorstep of our archaic world. But within our archaic world, these principles are themselves quite at home. They are not alien. They are fundamental to the original architecture of Earth. Mathematics and geometry are tools of construction that belong to nature and not exclusively to humans. The geometry we find within the layout of these structures is quite customary within the natural world. It is the will and lack of ritual that drive the construction that are abnormal.

The principles and precision within the designs of these temples are part of the fabric of the universe. Primitive life engages with that universe in an integral and unconscious way. This engagement does not involve understanding *how* it works, only that it *does* work. Scientists, on the other hand, claim that the 'success' of the human race is down to knowing as much as possible about *how* nature works so that we can play with it. But this claim has a flaw. Science is a product of conscious thought and linear time. Therefore, it is only able to analyze the single collapsed reality from which it has sprung. The physical sciences have placed us in a container and attached weights to our ankles. We can no longer perceive what may lie beyond its walls. We are only looking at the *inside* of the house. Three-dimensional space prevents us from realizing there is even an outside of the house, let alone a garden, neighbourhood and town. Consequently, we have a severely restricted understanding of how life in the cosmos really works.

From a primitive point of view, it is as if we had a severe bang on the head during the Neolithic period. We are suffering from *retrograde amnesia*. The moment we lost our memories, we also lost our intuitive understanding of universal natural law. We started to acquire and retain new knowledge from that moment, except that new knowledge is set in Time. We are re-learning the laws of the universe. We pass information down the generations in a long line of self-taught discoveries because we no longer have an innate sense of how it all works. This process has altered our perspective of the universe as we take notes and make adjustments to a world we now perceive of as a machine. Life has become a toy that we can take apart and experiment with. Of course, the other possible reason for our amnesia is that our species only arrived here in the Neolithic Age as the Sumerian and other myths point out. We have not evolved but have been engineered.

One of the glitches in this self-taught approach to learning about the universe is that we have developed a sense of owner-ship over the scientific principles and concepts we are discov-ering. We also consider that the ability to understand the why and how of natural phenomena brings nature under our con-trol, and only ours. We do not believe that there is any other force or vitality within nature to which we might be unseeingly subservient. We act as if brilliant humans created the quantum processes that exist in my laptop, when they are principles and states that exist independently within the wider universe. Bril-liant humans are merely finding out how to employ them.

Breakthroughs in science often begin with a logical hypoth-esis that scientists then endeavour to prove through mathemat-ics and experiment. This methodology, where we look for evidence of something we have already decided might be true, makes it easy for a simulation director to provide convincing explanations or evidence of what we think we are looking for.

We announce what we want to know, and we find it. Interestingly, illusionists use a similar technique to read people's minds. A magician asks us to think of a number between one and ten. But instead of scanning our minds for the number we are thinking of, they 'drop' a number into our minds before we have had time to think of one at all. We believe the number we arrive at is our own idea. We are oblivious to the influence of the illusionist. He or she guides our train of thought to a point where we believe we are having an original idea. In truth, they have steered us to that idea without our realizing it. We are unaware of any tampering, believing instead that our thoughts are the inspiration of an original and free-thinking mind. This type of psychological manipulation has been around for an extraordinarily long time, and it started in the Neolithic Age.

Look into my eyes

Keeping in mind this idea that we can be easily and unknowingly influenced, we need to identify what these builders *did* introduce to this dimension if it was not the technology with which they built the monuments. And what did they do to the primitive human psychology that caused such an irrevocable change to our understanding of primitive life? One thing is certain, the Proprietors and sorcerers who organized the building of the Neolithic monuments did not establish mathematical principles in this dimension. How could they if those principles were already here? What they did establish was an entirely new set of values and ideas: dominion, hierarchy, metrology, linearity, time, egoism, and, of course, the irreversible process of change. These concepts comprise the platform from which we are relearning about the universe, as they became embedded in our existence at the same time that these monuments were erected. For primitive life and minds, these traits are dangerous and offensive. They are deserving of immediate ostracism.

When we talk about sorcery, we are talking about the invisible and magical forces belonging to psychological manipulation. This is something we are often subject to in a civilized society. The principles of this manipulation originate in a primitive otherworld. As citizens belonging to a modern sociopolitical system, we are repeatedly assaulted by a variety of influences. Our education systems, politics, and media advise our behaviour. The relentless barrage of retail marketing and advertising guides our choices. We are also subject to the subtler but equally powerful social and emotional directions from our parents and everyone we know and love. It is up to us to decide what and how much of this onslaught of information and influence we accept or reject, but to be autonomous is impossible. These monuments are where this onslaught began. Strong imagery and powerful suggestion mesmerized primitive people into doing things it had previously been impossible for them to do.

The illusionist Derren Brown is someone who can control our behaviour in extraordinary ways, using imagery, misdirection, and the power of suggestion. He demonstrates psychological insight and a sharp mind in the way he selects an individual from a group and makes them do things that are quite shocking to those who are watching. He can convince people to eat raw onions as if they are apples, stick large needles through their hands, lose control of their limbs, and even believe they are living in a post-apocalyptic society where an unknown disease from outer space has turned everyone into zombies! Considering how modern humans revel at their control over personal thoughts, emotions, and decisions, this level of mesmerism is remarkable. In truth, the self-control we love to think we have is a bit of a fantasy. It is a desperate fantasy generated by our *lack* of control and by our subservience to a specific version of reality that is essentially artificial. We will continue to preserve this illusion as long as we do not question what our *primitive senses* present to us. In the previous chapter, we established that the Neolithic Revolution was where human instinct began breaking down. We did not discuss how. It was a process instigated by the dominant influence that was also responsible for the great monuments. The natural intuition with which Neolithic people detected disagreeable intentions began to corrode. Abnormal levels of coercion and duress followed.

Today we are awash with influence. All sorts of purveyors deliver their charms that they dress up in an assortment of veneers. They captivate us and weaken our instincts. But the real danger is that their temptations and suggestions do not relate to any meaningful code of conduct. Whether it is Derren Brown making us eat onions, a retailer selling products or friends giving advice, our minds are constantly subject to other people's insinuations. And there are no longer any rules. Yet we remain adamant that we are in control of our behaviour and the decisions we make. We demand freedom of speech and human rights. We behave as if we are not spellbound and submissive at all but assertive, confident, and in control. But if that were true, people would not spend money they do not have on things they do not need leading them into debt. People would not eat food they do not need to eat leading them to obesity and heart disease.[14] If we had full command of our minds, we would not act out scenarios like these, which only serve to make us unhappy and unwell.

We might say these people have a psychological disorder, but our ancient man would say they are mesmerized. Shadows influence them to buy the stuff and to eat the food, and so on. But more to the point is that they *allow* influences to affect them. Like Derren Brown's audience, they exhibit psychological loopholes that they no longer attend to and that the magician can exploit. Our ancient man would also point out that while we do not engage in the rituals around the figurative doorways of transformation, we are vulnerable to attack from influences in the otherworld, and indeed the sorcerers and advertisers in this one. In general, modern society does not recommend that we approach life with this primitive simplicity. Debt and consumption are fundamental principles that fuel our economies, (unlike the primitive gift economies that we talked about in Chapter 4), so retailers and advertisers will always encourage us to keep eating and keep buying. Neolithic farmers planted the seeds for these ideas, and now we are gathering the fruits.

---

[14] The average UK household owes £6,000 in unsecured borrowing and £54,000 including mortgages (November 2013, The Money Charity). Nearly two-thirds of men and women in the UK are overweight or obese (2013, Institute for Health and Metrics at the University of Washington).

Although Neolithic people's lives were simpler and their instincts were intact, the principle of psychological manipulation would have been the same as it is now. Back then, enchantment from spirits in the otherworld was quite normal; from fellow humans in this world, however, it was not. So how did these ancient sorcerers manage to get a foothold in a dimension where primitive nature had all the loopholes covered via ritualized behaviour?

The Proprietors: non-primitive people who have influence and the ability to manipulate. They set about constructing a new version of reality that they mesmerized primitive Neolithic people into accepting. This is what I believe we are witnessing in the megalithic monuments. They *manufactured* the non-ritualized penal colony that we now live in. Selfishness, greed, inequality, supremacy, and servility became the value-base for a new world. In this world, the place of ostracism and all the fear and isolation that accompanies it has been reworked so it is now an integral part of the fabric of reality. This fabric lies between a complex human environment and a sensitive and fragile ecosystem.

The primeval dimension of Earth is not innately constructed to accommodate this scenario so, in theory, it should not be happening, but it is. The primitive law of exclusion that automatically throws you out when you demonstrate negative traits, such as those brought by the Proprietors, no longer applies to human society. This situation may be acceptable for those who can toe this new line, but it is devastating for the masses that are excluded from society on grounds of poverty, mental illness or religion. It is certainly not OK for the natural world. Where is the protection for the innocent and well-in-tentioned when we sabotage nature's default security program in this way? It is comparable to the principle of vaccination. Doctors infect us with a small amount of a disease so that our bodies can build immunity to it, rather than ridding ourselves of the lifestyle that causes the disease to develop in the first place. In a similar way, mankind has engineered nature to accept unacceptable intentions and values. These monuments played a part in that engineering process.

Scores on the doors

Stonehenge has a different personality to those of the Middle Eastern ziggurats or Egyptian pyramids. Having said that, it was still built upon the same negative principles that oppose the original laws of this dimension. As we have already established, Stonehenge is not a passive, religious building innocuously marking the solstices and honouring the deaths of our ancestors. It is a strong statement of social and political authority. It demonstrates a power of a kind that was neat in Neolithic times. Whatever shifted the enormous stones into position was a force that was in the hands of an exclusive few. These people knew how to wield this force and according to a specific agenda. Imagine the impact this powerful imagery would have had on people whose animistic lives were steeped in images and their symbolic meaning. Its power would have been terrifying but perhaps also seductive and mesmerizing. Unlike today's government and religious buildings that have had the dominant principles with which we built them diluted through the ages,

Stonehenge in Neolithic Britain was a never-before-seen symbol of authority and prestige. Anyone in the vicinity would have been subject to that influence.

Stonehenge represents the beginning of a religious ideology that we recognize today in many ways. The act of worship as a social activity seems to have started here. It is Britain's first church. But it is important to note that Stonehenge, like the temple at Gobekli Tepe, was far more otherworldly than religious in its origins. We also need to consider that Neolithic Britain did not simply consist of newly developed farming communities all thinking, 'Oh, I wish we had thought of this sooner!' Resistance to these changes is likely to have been widespread, at least to start with. Stonehenge would have generated great suspicion and fear among local tribes. Standing as a strange and alarming image, tribal people would have run from it unless they were unfortunate enough for its spell to sweep them up. It was a strong spell. It was at the heart of profound sociopolitical changes in ancient Britain that we continue to live with today.

In the long barrows and burial tombs in the south of England and around Stonehenge we find evidence of this clash of worlds: extensive injury, malnutrition, and disease. These are clear signs of the hardship and suffering that these changes brought to the ordinary people of early Neolithic Britain.

In the tombs, we often find disarticulated human bones. This practice could be the result of a primitive fear of haunting. Perhaps people arranged and rearranged the bones of the dead to confuse the spirit of the deceased. Or perhaps they needed to guard the bones of loved ones from people who would want to use them in practices of necromancy or witchcraft. This could be a reason for building the stone chambers in the first place: for protection. It is a fragile argument that claims people built these tombs for ancestor worship as many experts testify. The key question we need answered is: why would tribes start building tombs and arranging bones to honour their ancestors, when death is a straightforward and everyday affair for tribal people who are not interfered with? The *need* to build these tombs, plus the unhappy state of the bones inside, once again denotes social anxiety and trauma rather than any spiritual devotion.

Let us imagine for a moment that we are primitive. We believe that when we die we transfer to another realm of existence. In this place, we meet our ancestors. Imagine now that this ancestral realm is the principal realm of existence. The earthly domain we occupy while we are 'alive' is but a stopping place on a much longer journey. Under these circumstances, any threat to the process of transformation when we die, any implication that there is a problem with the journey back to where we came from, would be immensely distressing. If we do not make it, we will become ghosts stagnating between worlds with the transformation incomplete. As Gilgamesh exclaims, 'The Snatchers have blocked my routes'. But his cries fall silently upon modern people who no longer understand the implications of what that means.

During these turbulent times, it is evident that people were anxious about gaining access to this ancestral realm. These tombs and strange rituals tell us that people were going to unusual lengths to ensure a passage through to the ancestors for those in their tribe who had died. The prehistoric people of

Britain would have engaged with the natural process of transformation at death, just as primitive people today still do. Our
ancient man would have done so too, albeit a million years earlier. It is a primitive tradition that knows no time. So what had
changed? Bearing in mind the primitive concerns about avoiding a bad death or a non-death, it is possible that the monumental architects were exploiting this fear. Perhaps those in charge
at Stonehenge were promoting the idea that via the monument
was now the *only* route to the ancestors after death. Could the
function of Stonehenge have been to manage, or to at least pretend to manage, this vital access to the afterlife? Anyone who
believed this chilling suggestion would have had no choice but
to visit the monument for the sake of their loved ones who had
died. In this way, the Stonehenge elite threatened primitive
people with the breakdown of the most sacred transformation
in their world. They were to become ghosts, the greatest primitive nightmare of all. If this is the case, then they were not *inventing* the afterlife, they were *controlling* it.

This theory fits with the political psychology of such a building. The formula for social hierarchy within human society of
any era involves those with power managing and regulating the
basic needs of the people, such as food, water, housing, and religion. In the case of Stonehenge (and other monuments), it included access to the ancestral realm at the point of death.

Part of the success of Stonehenge—the evidence for which
lies in the sheer numbers camped at Durrington Walls—was
that it did not advertise the fact that it was engineering the disruption. Instead, it presented itself as the solution. This is reminiscent of political and religious regimes at work right across

the world today. Many people find themselves part of a social system within which their lack of autonomy over their basic needs makes them vulnerable to whoever is in power. They are forced to ask for help from those who are responsible for managing the system. In so doing, they surrender further control to those in power who are then able to increase the pressure on a situation that they created in the first place. The welfare state is an example of this *social dependency* in the UK today. Making people dependent on a system that has itself engineered the impasse that subjects them to such dependency *without them noticing,* is an example of the sorcery practised by the elite at Stonehenge and indeed governments today. So we can conclude: misdirection was a Neolithic practice.

Resistance is futile

The earliest signs of activity in the location of Stonehenge date to around 7000 BCE. This tells us that it was an important site long before any stones arrived. Later on, once the stones were up, we know that people flocked to it like iron filings to a magnet. At Durrington Walls, we have evidence that from around 3000 BCE, thousands of people temporarily camped who we also know were *not* farming.

We have established that the dramatic changes to death and burial were not brought about by spiritual awakening but by crisis. Those in charge at Stonehenge were exercising considerable psychological power over the communities in the region. They appear to be persuading people in great numbers to abandon their usual ritual lives by inducing an epidemic of fear. This

Neolithic system of government sees the introduction of political and religious authority in Britain. Today, Christianity, Judaism, and Islam still use a similar 'promise of heaven' to incite certain values and behaviour in their devotees. The essence of this type of doctrine began with the prehistoric monuments. Before Stonehenge brought death and the afterlife to our attention, the transformation from life to the ancestral otherworld via death was a vital but quite ordinary affair, just as it still is for primitive people today. This point is invariably missing from most discussions about what the monument was for and why people built it.

Considering the disruption concerning death and the otherworld that we are uncovering, it is necessary to revisit another controversial subject: human sacrifice. Bearing in mind people have used humans and animals for sacrificial purposes throughout time, there is no reason not to explore this idea if there is evidence to suggest that there might be a case to answer. To start with, we need to be clear that human sacrifice at the site bears no relation to the druidic ceremonies that people associate with Stonehenge from the eighteenth century. I am referring to the practice of human sacrifice in a primitive context, whereby we give up something of value in order to benefit the community or tribe. In this case, it would have been the lives of human beings. The cremated remains of about sixty 'fairly healthy, fairly robust male individuals'[15] found in a burial pit

---

[15] Christie Cox, osteoarchaeologist at the University of Sheffield (taken from the TV production *Secrets of Stonehenge* with Professor Mike Parker Pearson).

next to Stonehenge are strong evidence to suggest human sacrifice took place there. Archaeologists say that they were aged between 25 and 40. They also tell us that these men were probably from a royal lineage. They do not tell us in what way they died or why they were buried together in a pit. Perhaps it is not possible to tell.

A Neolithic human sacrifice would have been an individual of considerable importance. Neolithic people, still underpinned by a primitive psychology, would have believed in the dynamism and qualities that a person demonstrated. Sacrificial objects would have been 'chosen' accordingly. The fact that the cremated remains were young males suggests that these men were warriors rather than royalty. Warrior males would have exhibited the cherished qualities for which their type was renowned—strength, courage, and vitality. These qualities made them eligible for sacrifice, much like the sacred white bulls of ancient Greece or the white horses of Rome. As men of the Neolithic era, humility, courage, and other primitive tribal qualities would still have been prevalent in these fighting men.

The sacrifice was likely to have taken place at winter solstice. As we talked about in Chapter 5, this is the most significant seam in sacrificial terms and we know the monument is perfectly aligned to honour that seam. The spirit of the 'victim'[16] would pass through to the otherworld and the gods or the

---

[16] The word *victim* comes from Latin *victima* meaning 'person or animal killed as sacrifice'. It was first recorded around the fifteenth century and used in a holy context. By the eighteenth century it had changed to mean 'a person who is oppressed by a power or situation'.

spirits therein would reciprocate in the form of good luck, prosperity, and protection. Those performing this ritual may also have implied that the sacrifice would sanctify the atmosphere as the qualities are released. Although this practice sounds gruesome to us, it would have been far more acceptable 5,000 years ago when people were still drenched in qualities, symbolism, and meaning. Only when we lose the significance of values and qualities, and the physical becomes the only focus of attention, does a human or animal sacrifice become merely an act of murder. Having said that, we would be naive to think that the Stonehenge elite would have had any volunteers for this task. But individuals chosen for sacrifice at this time are likely to have been treated with honour and esteem.

The so-called slaughter stone at Stonehenge may also have a connection to this ancient ritual. Its name derives from its dark red, blood-like colouring, which is unique to that particular stone. It gives the eerie impression that it has a memory of past events. It is not enough to say that its colour is caused by iron oxide when we are dealing with an ominous and animistic otherworld. The stone is lying flat in the main entrance to the causeway. The Neolithic Stonehenge management may have placed it there to unnerve those coming in and out of the circle, which was probably fenced. Most archaeologists assume that the stone was an upright that has fallen, but there is no evidence in the ground that this is the case. They admit the stone has been lying flat for a long time.

Primitive sacrifice honours gods or spirits via the act of giving up something that is important or exalted. According to primitive people, this act encourages good luck to enter their lives. When people carry it to an extreme, it is another sign that they are in crisis. Truly primitive people do not resort to such radical behaviour in their rituals as long as nothing disturbs their usual rituals and daily routines.

Human sacrifice at Stonehenge, if it occurred, is an example of the overlap between the primitive and civilized worlds that the Neolithic Revolution represents. The primitive: where communities made offerings and performed rituals to maintain tribal stability and harmony. The civilized: where elite designers and engineers held power and maintained control. The management at Stonehenge did not initiate these rituals to bring good luck to the thousands of people camped at Durrington Walls. They wanted to mesmerize and so rule them.

Go west

In order to understand a little more about the miracle of Stonehenge's engineering, we need to think primitively. We know now that this means looking at the stones in terms of qualities instead of seeing them as things. The smaller bluestones—the original stones at the site—came from the Preseli Mountains in the far west of Wales. The qualities of the direction of the West would have radiated from these stones. Long before they became geographical bearings, the four cardinal directions existed as impressive and dynamic qualities. Within those qualities we find the reasons for the stones' significance during these times.

In myth, the West is associated with death as the sun descends into the western horizon every evening. Water is also associated with the West, and in the Preseli region there are over two hundred natural springs. Within the spirit of water, we find emotion and the power of memory. In the classical Greek myths, Mnemosyne is the goddess of memory and time.[17] She presides over the rivers of memory and forgetfulness in the underworld, where souls are invited to drink from one or the other after death. Even modern scientists are perplexed by the phenomenon of the 'magnetic memory of water' in relation to electromagnetic radiation (EMR). They have proved that water treated with EMR retains the memory of the radiation for some time afterwards. They consider this to be impossible because the structure of water should not allow it to store these effects.

As Neolithic animists, we would believe the stones to possess these potent westerly and watery attributes. Therefore, as modern observers, we might assume that the people who quarried and moved them wanted to employ the Spirit of the West. This would include its influence and authority in matters of death and memory. It is clear that the perpetrators intended to exploit what was fundamentally important to primitive people. They wanted to disrupt what was integral to tribal perception and understanding. Together with powerful imagery, they used the animistic language that primitive ancient people understood so well.

The points we have discussed so far in this chapter—sorcery, psychological manipulation, social disruption, and human sacrifice—are adding up to Stonehenge looking less and less like a fancy cemetery. It now looks like a political tool designed to manipulate primitive minds by introducing an unreasonable

---

[17] and the inventor of language and words.

fear of death to their psychology. The smaller bluestones arrived at the site from Wales around 3000 BCE. The monumental sarsen doorways followed them about five hundred years later, creating the theatrical monument we find at the site today.

While the impossible engineering of these ancient monuments is intriguing from a physical perspective, their original function—whatever we believe it to be—is now redundant. Today they exist as archaic souvenirs depicting the irreversible and tragic hardening of our world. They are symbols of the rigidity that our perception of reality now endures, including that of our bodies and our spirits. The world we live in now is cast-iron, unbreakable. It is a world where we reduce the substance, intelligence, and charm of a prehistoric human to a set of bones, a DNA sample, and a cranial capacity. The delicate image of our ancient man was made only of nature's principles before he became an 'evolutionary dead-end'. I believe that these monuments too were once apparitions of a digital quality. They consisted of values and principles before they also collapsed into immovable heaps of stone. If we perceived matter as a malleable and sensuous fabric that created images rather than things, sorcerers could easily have moved the stones up and down, across great distances and into impossible arrangements. Primitive minds would have watched in awe. But these minds were not impressed with the physical weight that the sorcerers lifted because there was no physical weight as such. It was the creation or recreation of the sacred portals through which they would travel to the afterlife that amazed them. Elite groups were breaking the laws of this primitive dimension. They were gaining power and status through their ability to manipulate nature, primitive minds, and the very fabric of this world.

Considering this, it is amusing to imagine the magicians at Stonehenge looking on at the twenty-first century. What would they have thought of the experimental archaeologists with their log-rolling devices attempting to heave forty-tonne stones across Salisbury Plain, as if that was what *they* did?

All that is gold does not glitter

All sorts of controversial theories exist about how and why ancient people built Stonehenge and other monuments. Some believe that the Great Pyramids resemble ancient machines or even generators of some kind. Others believe that Neanderthal-Cro-Magnon hybrids built the Gobekli Tepe temple. But what we are quite sure they all shared is an association with death and the afterlife.

The personalities of the Egyptian pyramids and their pharaohs are altogether different from the bureaucratic Sumerians and the mysterious, watery British. The glamorous Egyptians presented the Hollywood version of catastrophic change: stylish, glitzy, good-looking, dripping with opulence, and larger than life. Despite their showiness, the principles that we see introduced in Egypt are the same as at every other monumental site. The gods, the pharaohs, the ruling class, however we choose to refer to these beings were arrogant, self-indulgent, and domineering. They inundated the region with traits incompatible with its primitive origins. Inevitably, slavery followed. Like the Stonehenge monument, the powerful images of the pyramids would have played a big part in the social conditioning of the people. In fact, they visually represented the new hierarchy that the Egyptians introduced at this time.

The pharaohs paraded before their people as if they were gods. This tells us as primitive psychologists that we are dealing with individuals who wanted to exercise authority over the ordinary people who revered such gods. Presenting 'cultural evolution' as an explanation for this huge shift in human behaviour is rather vague. To say that an Egyptian pharaoh is descended from once primitive hunters does not make sense. We can find no remnants of a primitive ethos: no manners, humility, equality or cooperation. They demonstrate only a vast rational intelligence, political ruthlessness, and an unerring sense of vanity. These attributes do not belong in a natural, primitive world, and they spill from every 2.5 tonne, perfectly placed brick of the Pyramids of Giza. Combined with nature's principles of mathematics and geometry, and her dreamlike imagery, the pharaohs produced these monuments. All over the world at this time, various elite groups were using nature's geometric blueprints to generate a colossal change in the natural systems of life in this dimension. But they were breaking so many rules, and they broke them to such an extent, there was no way it was going to end well.

In a world where there is no weight and we only have imagery there are no longer mysteries around how people erected the sandstone blocks at Stonehenge or how they placed a giant sarcophagus into the Great Pyramid when it was too big to fit through the door. Where there is no geography and we only have imagery, we no longer wonder about how the bluestones travelled hundreds of miles to Wiltshire or how early modern humans appeared in France as if out of nowhere. Where we have shrewd, elite groups managing portals through which we cross dimensions, transformation, including death at the end of life, becomes disrupted. But as these sorcerers were busy performing their great feats of illusion across the Neolithic world, the classical laws of physics were ultimately being born. Perhaps they went too far or on for too long, playing with the imagery of natural shapes, patterns, and coordinates. Eventually, their extraordinary experiments collapsed. Nature withdrew her gentle charms, and the rigid principle of measurement began its rule.

All over Egypt quarries were abandoned. Statues and monuments were left unfinished as the stone simply became too heavy to lift. Three dimensions, their dynamic laws, and linear time finally carved out the dimensional reality we recognize today. Stonehenge froze to the spot where we now find it. By the Iron Age, the site was completely empty of people. It was no longer a manoeuvrable, digital weapon of command but a pile of cold, hard stones. For the first time, as depicted in all these monuments worldwide, we have examples of previously inconceivable physical endurance and permanence. It was nature's turn to act. She removed the dreamlike and mythical qualities with which this remarkable imagery had been created. The natural spirits retreated and the remaining portals to the otherworld were sealed shut. It was a Neolithic wind that changed thousands of years ago as these monuments solidified. The aftermath of the atrocities executed by these sorcerers became cemented in time.

Stars in their eyes

Within the ancient cultures that practised megalithic architecture, we often find a connection to the stars. The three we have brushed upon—Neolithic Britain, Sumer, and Egypt—all have monuments or myths that associate their gods with the heavens. Let us take the perpetrators of these radical new cultures out of the picture for a moment and return to the primitive people who were in residence before they arrived. These people's lives were bound to the natural world. The stars above them played significant roles as the original authorities who presided over life and death. In traditional cultures, people associated stars with ancestors. Many tribes see their ancestors in the sky looking over them; the Bushmen call them 'the eyes of the dead'. Gods and ancestors guide them from the heavens. It is a place of great influence. It is the source of what they are, and where they must return to when they die. Certainly in prehistoric times, when there was no light pollution and when the stars were closer to us, we would have related to them differently, more intimately. When humans live without geography, they consider that whatever lies ten miles away on land to be more mysterious than the stars that are above them every night and moving across the sky in familiar patterns. These constellations have distinct personalities which we find in ancient astrology, alchemy, and myths. They have been influencing native people for thousands, perhaps millions of years.

Many of the great stone monuments are aligned with the heavens. Therefore, it is not hard to imagine a vitality residing within the patterns in the night sky, one that is unfamiliar to us but which was well known to those alive at that time. Experts tell us that the three pyramids at Giza are aligned with the constellation of Orion. Is there a compelling influence emanating from those stars that affects those structures, even today? (This would be the same influence that ancient astrologers associate with the indigenous *djinn* spirits). This kind of otherworldly potency left our realm of perception a long time ago. But perhaps a little evidence of it remains in the fact that modern building surveyors and structural engineers cannot explain how under the weight of six million tonnes of limestone and granite we do not see these structures subsiding into the desert sand.

Similarly, Stonehenge is aligned to the winter solstice and drawing from the sun, our very own star. The daily cycle of the sun is at the root of the modern twenty-four-hour day. The solidification of these monuments has assisted the process of turning that most primeval ritual into a linear sequence. Stonehenge is configured for the winter solstice sunlight to enter through a doorway. The perfect quality of gold midwinter light travels from the otherworld where the primitive sun resides to the collapsed physical world in which we reside. In modern times, we interpret the monument's alignment as a show of reverence to the sun as a powerful deity. But from a truly primitive point of view, it is demonstrating something a little more underhand.

We know that the solstices are important seams in nature that ritualize the transformation between life and death, beginning and end. The stone doors are symbolic of the portals within those seams. This alignment forces the transformation of the sun into three-dimensional time and space as it passes through the door. No one had done this before *on purpose.* This is *not* sun-worship. We find primitive reverence of the sun demonstrated in the ritual of birth, growth, and death, just as we see in the changing seasons and the protesting blackbird. As we watch the sun rise on winter solstice morning and break through one of these ancient doorways, we are witnessing the controlled capture of the qualities within the transformation itself.

Let us continue with the idea that some sort of quality or *vimna* from the stars was helping to fuel these changes taking place on the ground. From this perspective, the Stonehenge ritual illustrates how those involved were attempting to seize the *vimna* of the sun and use it to energize their strange new activities. The subsequent collapse has forced this process to repeat itself each year and, in so doing, has activated linear time. Winter solstice is now an annual event. We have tagged the solstice sunlight like we tagged the seagull, which has set it within geography and time. This places the otherworldly light within a set of circumstances that it should never be exposed to. But the sun, like the seagull, does not take on this geography. He continues with the primitive ritual of birth, growth, and death, oblivious to our physical laws even though we have subjected him to them. The end result is that we who live on *this* side of the collapsed door no longer see the sun in his animistic or godly form. Instead, we have a copy created according to the mechanics of this world. The sun is now a giant ball of gas and hot plasma residing 93 million miles away from Earth, whose light takes eight minutes to reach us travelling at 186,000 miles per second. 'He' becomes 'it'. Science has replaced the otherworld, and scientists the gods.

The geometry of imagery

We cannot talk about nature's geometry without briefly mentioning crop circles. These extraordinary apparitions also seem to be linked to the art of image manipulation that the prehistoric architects used for their building projects. Crop circles are geometric patterns that appear, very suddenly, in crops often near ancient settlements such as hill forts and stone circles. These patterns are perfect illustrations of nature's innate rapport with mathematics and precision. In the fields of southern England every summer, those principles reveal themselves to the bewilderment of farmers, scientists, and journalists. Whether we believe they are the creations of aliens, starry beings or some other force, we know that (mostly) they are not man-made. They break the same physical rules that the Pyramids and Stonehenge do. They are symbolic of universal principles that *apply* in this three-dimensional world. But according to our physical laws, they should not appear so suddenly or precisely in a field of wheat or corn. They bring stories and messages, ones we do not really understand, and they defy our solidified existence entirely.

The mathematical precision of a crop circle has a starry quality. They often depict celestial relationships: constellations and planets, the sun and the moon. These images convey timelessness. Their geometry is so fundamental to the structure of nature that they could have been designed a million years ago or half an hour ago. Many appear in Wiltshire and in particular around Stonehenge.

This symbol is one of the oldest in the world. It appears in caves and on natural, rocky outcrops, ancient monuments and megaliths the world over. They date from the Upper Palaeolithic right up to the Bronze Age. We also find it in mythology representing an eye or seeing, or as an image of the sun. We find a reworked version of it within the ancient Chinese yin yang symbol of infinite balance. It is a common shape for some of the simple crop circles as well as forming the basis for many of the more complex circles. It also resembles the aerial view of a Neolithic causewayed enclosure and earthworks.

Causewayed enclosures consist of one to four concentric ditches with an internal bank. Crossing the ditches at intervals are causeways that give the monuments their names. There are 70 causewayed enclosures in southern Britain alone, 100 in France and more across Europe. Many henges, including Stonehenge, started life as one.

Although our ancient man did not make this mark, he inherently knew what it meant. It symbolized the source, the template, from which he drew his understanding about life and *vimna*. The dot at the centre is the place to which the sun travels every night and from which the stars come out and shine. It is where oak trees go when they die and the source of the wind as it blows gently across our ancient man's camp. It is where the flame goes when a Pirahã blows out a candle. As I have said so many times already, in this place there is no time. After all, where in the circle around the point would you mark a million years?

We could say that this is *the* symbol of primitive life. So why does it appear carved in so many places that are to do with death? Caves, portals, burial passages and tombs, standing stones and dolmen relate to death and the afterlife or the otherworld. Across Britain, there are rocks and megaliths covered with cup and ring marks depicting this symbol. Some have more concentric rings, sometimes up to eight or nine. Often accompanying these symbols are similar marks that carry a significant addition—what experts call a tail. This is a straightish line that runs from the centre through most or all of the circles. It clearly depicts linear time running amok through the timelessness of the natural cycles.

These are ancient expressions. Perhaps the marks were depicting what people were in the process of losing. The simplicity that lies within the circle and the dot was devastated in the Neolithic period as complexity, bogus gods, and unethical principles forced themselves upon an innocent, primeval landscape. These marks are either a warning or a curse. It is hard to tell whether they promote or oppose what was happening. Either way, they are symbols depicting the drama of a changing world. Our experience of life transformed from a circle with a centre to a line with no end. Imagine our ancient man waking up from a dream and finding this petrified physical reality. He would think that *this* must be the dream because it is a nightmare.

CHAPTER 11

The Paradoxical Machine

'This is the way the world ends;
Not with a bang but a whimper.'
T S Eliot

It appears that engineered beings, bogus gods, pharaohs, and sorcerers, or, in less dramatic terms, those non-primitive beings who 'appeared' and introduced civilized principles to Earth, were engineering a perception of reality for their own ends. They implemented what we now know of as the physical world: a measured and collapsed universe. This world comprises three spatial dimensions—up and down, side to side, back and forth—from which there are no apparent exits. Accompanying these physical dynamics is continuous time. This is the method by which we can measure the 'bits in between', those that are the inevitable results of travelling from spatial point A to spatial point B. These beings were the inventors of the arrow of time, the very concept of linearity. They were responsible for the devastation brought about by progress and change which that concept enabled. These physical laws are illusions we now live with and accept. They are tools engineered and managed by those who live without time (and therefore without having to spend time travelling from A to B), in order to influence a particular way of perceiving *an environment.* In so doing, these beings did not eradicate the delicate and ritualistic way of life Earth's occupants once enjoyed, but simply rendered it invisible. We can no longer register its presence.

Time will tell

My laptop aptly demonstrates the illusion of linearity. Right now, it is busy typing this document for me and providing the impression that there are hundreds of pages that exist before the one I am currently working on. But where are all those pages? While I am not working on them, they are nowhere. For my computer the centre, namely the place of action, is all that is relevant, much like life in a primitive tribe. In order to accommodate my linear psychology, the various applications on my laptop provide me with a scroll bar that allow me to cope with all the backwards and forwards I believe I have to perform. They are designed to provide this service for me because I am unaware of being able to work in any other way. Unlike computers and all life within a primitive nature, I cannot manage *life at the centre* because my psychology is not structured to see or experience life in this way. The geographical map used by my laptop to save and retrieve files is merely an illusion designed solely for my benefit.

Ever since the invention of computers, philosophers and computer scientists have debated whether free will and conscious thought are elements of the human psyche that we can introduce to a machine. But it turns out to be our linear psychology that makes modern human intelligence and machine intelligence incompatible. In fact, the way that computers have to accommodate our linear thinking suggests they might have more in common with a primitive human world than we do.

The Neolithic period saw time put into action. The road we are travelling now was an idea that the Proprietors planted in the human mind. As well as time, they planted other non-primitive ideas: measurement, progress, quantity, weight, geography, and so on. We could imagine that the stones of the Neolithic stone circles were not erected but also planted. An influence was farmed. Agriculture was not the utilitarian revolution we believe it to be, but a psychological take-over of the primitive mind. Social revolutionaries employed the natural process of birth, growth, and death to cultivate civilized ideas and grow them into substantial principles and concepts that now serve our modern lifestyle. This leads us to conclude with the realization that mankind's obsession with material survival is in fact the *effect* of civilizing, and not the cause as our textbooks lead us to believe.

In the previous chapter, we discussed the appearance of the powerful beings that were driving these catastrophic changes. Now we need to ask the question: where did they go? What became of the kings and queens of Mesopotamia, Egypt, and Stonehenge? Evidence of these supreme beings appears to dwindle as time passes. They seem to have disappeared as abruptly as they had arrived. Perhaps they returned to wherever they had come from in the first place, abandoning mankind to its three-dimensional fate.

But this is not quite the end of the story. These spurious gods are clever, enough even to exit time and live beyond it, rather like the director of an ancestor simulation lives outside the simulation itself. Perhaps they remain in their discrete other world, watching and waiting—but waiting for what? To be resurrected, reintroduced? A long time ago they interrupted an established and successful pattern of primitive existence on Earth by introducing a closed loop of perpetual motion: we call it Time. The result: progress is now running out of control. Civilization has removed all the primitive people who would conflict with progress and change. So with no resistance and with no idea of what lies beyond the limits of this loop, the illusion can continue indefinitely. It must be only a matter of time, literally, until progress makes a quantum leap into a new phase, which may well include these so-called gods once again.

Egyptian mummification, which dates from a similar time to Stonehenge, is another example of extreme death rituals that appeared seemingly out of nowhere. Many writers see the immortal treatment of these royal bodies as the Egyptian ruler's denial of mortality. They attempted to defy the mortal laws that normal humans are subjected to, engineering a privileged passage for themselves through to the afterlife. Considering these beings, along with their Sumerian cousins, were responsible for introducing the concept of mortality to this dimension in the first place, we can assume that they would want to avoid it themselves. However, the extent to which they go is somewhat extreme. First, they embalmed the body with chemicals that delayed decomposition. Then, they wrapped each part of the body in bandages after having removed certain internal organs which they placed in jars. Next, they adorned the body with protective amulets before placing it in an airtight sarcophagus. The sarcophagus was then assigned to an impenetrable place, such as a chamber deep inside a giant pyramid that was impossible for mere mortals to reach. To finish, they sealed everything in and placed a curse upon anyone who would disturb it. As a psychologist, I would describe the excessive nature of this behaviour as intensely paranoid and obsessive. In the case of the ancient Egyptians, we cannot dismiss such paranoia as merely cultural or religious without finding a more specific motivation for it.

Considering the emphasis on preserving the body within these burial rituals, we can imagine that the pharaohs had a desire to come back to life at a time in the future when genetic engineering, molecular cloning, and hybridization are available to an exclusive few—again. Perhaps they hid their mummified bodies away to last the entire passage of time so that they can reintroduce them when we run out of time and start a new chapter, as we are about to do.

In this vein, mummification would have been the precursor to modern day cryonics. There are cryopreservation institutes in Europe and America that preserve human bodies after legal death has been declared. They use low-temperature preservation techniques to prevent decomposition with a view to resuscitating the body at some point in the future. At the moment, we do not know when that point will be as the technology does not exist yet, but the service is currently available to anyone who can afford the six-figure price tag. One of the oldest mummies we know of is a severed head found in South America dating to 3500 BCE. It is comparable to a process called neuro-preservation, which is a distinct version of cryonics where only the head is preserved for possible future cloning.

Perhaps we may never advance molecular cloning far enough to ever resurrect an Egyptian pharaoh in this way. And more to the point, why would we ever want to? But by comparing intentional mummification to the process of modern cryonics we gain more of an idea about the *motivation* behind such extreme behaviour. What it tells us is that the Egyptians are demonstrating a desire to come back to life *on Earth* in the future, rather than ensuring they have a safe journey to the eternal afterlife. If we have identified their intention to return to this dimension at a particular time, we can only imagine how they might engineer that process if they once existed beyond whatever we believe reality to be today.

Techno-portals

On the flipside of this idea—that there are ancient beings existing beyond this reality waiting for the right moment to re-join us—our intrepid scientists are nearing the edge of our own revolution in perception. We are about to leave this reality altogether. The discovery of how to cross dimensions underpins this leap in development. Science is looking for the elusive exits from our three dimensions and plans to move us through them. Quantum and computer scientists have long been aware that they will meet the physical limitations of this material world at some point. That point seems to have arrived. Computational capacity, which has so far doubled every two years according to the predictions of Moore's Law, will soon be unable to advance any further without hitting an invisible wall. As we approach the physical limits associated with matters of matter, the classical laws of physics tell us that we must cross a dimensional threshold into a world where those laws do not apply.

Many disciplines within science are working on this particular problem. Professor Andrew Dzarak,[18] one of the world's leading quantum computer scientists, disclosed the closeness of this dimensional revolution in 2012 when he announced the successful development of embedding a quantum state within a silicon chip. 'Imagine if you could start building your own molecule or your material on a computer and then completely simulate its behaviour.'[19]

Futurist and Google director Ray Kurzweil in his book *The Singularity Is Near* refers to 'the law of accelerating returns'. He explains how the exponential rate at which technology is developing indicates that this dimensional shift is a lot closer than we think. He goes on to hypothesize that by 2020, we will have enough processing power at our disposal to simulate a whole human brain. Individuals will be able to exist forever as digital avatars. By 2045, he predicts the Singularity will transpire. At that point, events will occur that will exceed our ability to comprehend them. The human race will be launched into a new

---

[18] Scientia Professor at the University of New South Wales, Centre for Quantum Computation and Communication Technology.

[19] New York Times 29th September 2012.

phase of existence. We will have a billion times more computational power at our disposal than all the human brains alive today, but will have lost the ability to control it. When this occurs, it will be a true revolution in that it will be irreversible.

As human beings, we should all take an active interest in these developments. Once we have crossed over into a quantum, limitless world, we will not be able to return to the way we experience life now. We will finally move through that portal, and it will close behind us. A completely new perceived reality is dawning on mankind. This is how it was for the primitive hunters of the Neolithic Revolution, when their dreamlike world solidified before their eyes and life became filled with bizarre hazards that they could not compute. Considering the irrevocable transformation that artificial intelligence, molecular computing, and biotechnology will initiate, these developments are presenting us with a similar state of affairs. As we hurtle towards this seam, the irony is that we will enter a timeless and, therefore, ancient world but without possessing the primitive values and psychology required to exist within it.

Even for conventional computers, information processing does not involve three dimensions. There are no miles or kilometres that the information contained in my laptop is required to travel. The World Wide Web does not employ the cardinal directions and, thanks to social media and video communication, we no longer socialize predominantly in three dimensions, but in two. For now, we remain on the outside looking in. But as we interact with our personal computers, consoles, and smartphones, we witness the miracle of time condensing down to something so tiny that it becomes non-time, yet we do not acknowledge how incredible that is. Via these gadgets, the cumbersome world of real-time has quantum magic piercing through it from other worlds where time hardly exists at all. As I type these words on my laptop, my fingers and the words that materialize on the screen are synchronized. If I enter sums into my spreadsheet, the correct answers appear in an instant, as if by a trick or a charm. This is how the quantum principles work in a computer. When we interact with them, we do not notice they are there. We accept their unearthly nature because we are busy doing something else like writing, surfing, liking or tweeting. As this technology is hidden in the fabric of our everyday lives, we do not question its absurd existence. In fact, we do not think about it at all.

So, when we find that elusive portal and enter this multi-dimensional quantum universe, the odds are that we are not going to notice that either. This is a significant element of the enchantment we are under. It will not be a case of walking boldly into a brave new world like little Lucy walks through the wardrobe into the brilliance and wonder of Narnia. It is more likely that we will not know it has happened. The danger of constantly moving away from the original template of life on Earth is that our primitive senses which once assessed *intention* have stopped working. We do not use them, so they have stopped functioning. But if we want to intervene with what happens next to our species, we must bring those primitive senses and principles back to life again.

The dangers of simulating immortality

As scientists advance technology towards quantum computing, simulated environments, and synthetic life forms, there are also reports of developments in digital immortality. Whole brain emulation, or mind uploading, is a 'radical new form of human enhancement' (Sandberg & Bostrom 2008). In theory, uploading involves scanning a brain to a computerized substrate so it will behave like the original mind as a perfect copy. Accompanying this digital mind may be a mechanical or biotech hybrid form, and eventually a simulated environment. From this platform, it appears that civilized humans will not be required to overcome their fear of dying after all.

The Russian billionaire Dmitry Itskov set up the 2045 Initiative in 2011. It is a research effort that claims to introduce mankind to a holographic avatar by the year 2045.[20] We will have a reinvented and immortal human existence, and all for the price of a new car. He says, 'This project is leading down the road to immortality...People don't want to die.'[21] Scientists in Britain at the University of Reading are also hoping to upload a human brain into a robot within the next ten years.

The approach to this research tells us that the scientists and investors in posthumanism, whatever their particular discipline or slant on the future of humanity, are agreeing on two fundamental assumptions. First, they are relying on the materialist idea that the spirit or awareness of every person resides within the synapses and electrical connections of their physical

---

[20] Oddly, the same year as the onset of Kurzweil's Singularity.

[21] Wired.com 29 February 2012.

brain. When the body dies, we die completely. There is no soul or consciousness that travels or transcends when we have finished with the biology. If they have got this wrong, we have a considerable problem on our hands.

The second critical factor is that they do not consider that the natural world possesses an intention other than what biologists and chemists can explain. To continue in this regard is to continue with the problems we currently experience in relation to the perceived chaos of nature. After all, African lions do not *think* they are searching for nitrogen, just as seagulls do not know they 'possess exocrine glands located in supraorbital grooves of the skull by which sodium chloride can be excreted through the nostrils to assist the kidneys in maintaining electrolyte balance'.[22] The laws pertaining to biology and chemistry are tools with which humans manipulate their environment. They do not exist for the rest of the natural world. If we do not accept wild nature as a wilful entity in its own right, we disregard the very root of human existence, not as spiritual or conscious beings, but as animals on this planet who reside within nature's jurisdiction. Within the new digitized existence, how is nature's vitality—or *vimna*—going to feature? Will we be bereft of any relationship with the natural world and so become purely artificial or will we weave nature into the life support so it exists behind the scenes as it does now? Both of these scenarios present problems.

---

[22] Wikipedia article: title 'Gull', subtitle 'Diet and feeding'.

At first glance, the former does not seem possible. If we do not include nature in the equation then where is the initial trigger for life going to come from? Throughout these developments, this issue remains an anomaly that scientists struggle to resolve. Nature must feature somewhere for us to be able to know life at all, even if it is within a computer program. Earth, air, fire, and water, before they were physical substances were important natural properties. Together, they made up physical life in an unmeasured primeval world. In an unmeasured technological world, how will we survive without them?

The latter scenario, whereby we only weave structural threads of nature into the new platform of reality, suggests that not much will change compared to how our relationship stands at the moment. We treat nature like it is a machine: plant and grow, plant and grow, and so on. But the predictability of nature's function, such as we see in the principle of growth, is not absolute by any means. We experience this fact most dramatically in extreme weather, climate change and crop failure, widespread psychiatric illness and physical disease. *Nature* has imposed these anomalies upon mankind, and we have limited means of effectively controlling them. How, then, will such volatility and devastation manifest within a mind emulation or a simulated world where we have simply transferred our failure to understand nature's laws from one platform to another? How do we think we might control nature's wild and unpredictable personality in the future if we cannot control it now? Without speaking her primitive, animistic language, she is likely to continue as a turbulent and unstable factor. She is a loophole that scientists are not addressing because they do not believe there is a loophole to address. The truth is, as long as we leave out animism and the primitive otherworld—the myth, symbolism, and ritual—then our control over nature will always be full of hidden cracks and faults. Civilization cannot live with nature but it cannot live without her either.

One thing we do know, when the technocrats refer to 'species typical' emulations, they are referring to a civilized mind. Ironically, this is a mind whose psychology is not compatible with the immaterial existence they intend to lock it into. Scientists and philosophers are talking about entering a world where a primitive mind would be superior. A timeless, non-physical and non-linear dimension belongs to nature. As modern materialists, we do not understand what that means in practice. A primitive mind is indiscernible from its environment; it blends by relating and empathizing. This is the nature of primitive animism and seeing the spirit or intention in everything around you. This is also what happens in dreams, where the impenetrable make-up of our environment is not present. Again, we communicate with instinct and imagery, and without all the 'bits in between'. This is also what we find in a quantum system, where the laws of cause and effect do not apply. Instead, particles interconnect via patterns, probabilities, and relationships. The synchronicity of my fingers and words on my laptop and the synchronicity of the starlings and the seagulls are the same. My laptop and the birds adhere to nature's *integrity principle*. The only place that is devoid of this timeless relationship is the solid reality we perceive. This version of reality adheres to concocted laws that exclude us from our surroundings, not only because of its dense molecular construction, but also because we *believe* it all to be dead. On the other hand, the microscopic world of quantum physics tells us that the world we live in is made of principles that are not dense and impenetrable. Dynamic and constantly moving miniscule particles are at the heart of the rigid, dead table that I am sitting at.

I am animist, therefore I am

Let us for a moment imagine that there is the potential for life in all things. Now, let us extend that to our faithful and hardworking computers. As animists, the computers, like a sunbeam or a rock in a primitive world, would gain a massive injection of intention. This would result in the relationship becoming a two-way street: the computers *interacting* with us rather than merely passively receiving our instructions. In this way, all our gadgets would inherit what we might call a spirit—an intention that is not conscious like ours but one that is not dead and non-reciprocal in the way we assume machines to be. In a primitive sense, they would 'take in' aspects of what we deliver to them via our everyday interface. We learn from them, but moreover, they would learn from us as they absorb who we are and what we do. In turn, they influence and inform us on how they work and what they are. We influence one another. I have based this scenario on the primitive template of life. It is only from a world view deficient of animism, which the likes of Newton and Darwin helped to forge, that we would not consider this to be happening.

Ironically, computer scientists and developers of AI are striving to develop exactly this: a thinking computer that can learn, enhance, interact, and adapt organically and even consciously within its physical parameters. But how do we know that computers are not already doing something like this on an animistic level that we are not aware of? Considering our inability to perceive or understand animism, how can we be sure that computers are not learning from us even now? Perhaps the human mind and the machine mind are engaging in some form of primitive reciprocation according to natural law as we speak. We might then wonder if the artificial intelligence programs designed to pass a Turing test[23] have the reverse effect: they are influencing humans to behave like them. Are we making the machines in our likeness or are they making us in theirs? Turing tests inevitably spark debates around what exactly 'intelligence' and 'understanding' are. Without a definition, how are we able to recognize them in our machines? But what if the nature of *human* intelligence is such that we are unable to recognize a particular type of understanding or intention that the machines possess and are busy utilizing without us noticing?

At the heart of the problem with testing machines for intelligence is anthropomorphism. We want to test computers for their ability to have their own mind, to think for themselves. But if we think in terms of animism, we do not impose human traits onto the idea of intentionality. Then we have to consider that a machine might possess a vitality that we are unable to detect because it is *not* human, just as we are unable to detect it in a rock or a hill. So it is not a question of whether the machines are thinking or feeling in a similar way to humans but

---

[23] A test designed to assess a machine's capacity to behave as a human.

whether they are taking part in an ancient law, one we have been conditioned to believe does not exist.

It is interesting that this scenario evades the issue of moral responsibility which would otherwise arise from finding out that machines have an intention outside of their programming. Civilized society is alone in its need for morality. Machines adhere to primitive law, where right and wrong exist as logical states and not as ethical distinctions between decency and depravity. This is the same for a tree as it grows and for a primitive person interacting with their tribe. Machine intelligence will not overwhelm the human race because it has misplaced intentions; that is how *we* work. It will take over because we have allowed the principles of hierarchy, dominion, and progress to rule our lives. Machine supremacy will merely become a logical step in a sequence of events. It is another link in the chain of human evolution that we have engineered.

Hubert Dreyfus was a philosopher of AI in the second half of the last century. He suggested that human intelligence is less to do with the symbolic manipulation performed by our brains and more to do with a primeval instinct and intuition. This is an unusual opinion and one that I share, but which today holds little water. However, Dreyfus was able to start such a discussion on the grounds that we can loosely relate to the intuitive behaviour he talks about. Scientists understand his argument even if they do not agree that his 'primacy of intuition' is what defines intelligence. But to have a discourse about machines and humans communicating in an animistic way is impossible. To experience the intention in an object we interact with such as a leaf, a moonbeam or a computer is not something we can relate to. It is an infantile notion. Therefore, no scientist will consider animism or intentionality as relevant to AI, even though they are as innate to the primitive psyche as instinct and intuition.

An immaculate conception

So, if the very machines we have designed and built are mesmerizing us to behave like them, our next question might be: how and why is this happening? In search of an answer, we inevitably start to look for a Creator.

In terms of an ancestor simulation, we are back thinking in terms of linear time. We imagine that there is something beyond the simulation positioned in the future that is controlling it and us. We also think of our descendants as human beings, like us but a little more advanced. But neither one of these ideas is necessarily true. If we know time is a state of mind and not an objective reality, then for a Creator it may not exist. Therefore, he is unlikely to reside in the future if there is no such thing. With regard to the humanness of our Creator, this is also looking doubtful.

At the other end of our creation, of course, is our extinction. At the hands of a superintelligence or 'strong superhumanity' (Bostrom 2004), which scientists are currently working on, we could soon be met with the end of our species. Computer scientists describe superintelligence as a hypothetical entity that possesses intelligence beyond that of any existing human being. We find it in the context of AI, genetic engineering, and computational neuroscience. The development of this research inspires a host of philosophical questions, which at present remain mostly unanswered.

There are theorists who worry that once we bring this superintelligence to life, much of humanity will become obsolete. The current structure of our society is not compatible with the sort of world that intelligence of this kind would exist within. Its people will serve no function and so are likely to be discarded. After all, with no need for shops, who needs shopkeepers? With no need for infrastructure, who needs builders, engineers, farmers, accountants, solicitors, and so on. Social, political, and economic change beyond our comprehension would ensue, which takes us right back to the events of the Neolithic Revolution. Who needs hunters when I can grow crops? Who needs the social equality of a tribe when I can own land, grow my own food, live longer, and strive for a better life? Yet we know that civilization does not deliver quality of life or liberty to the vast majority of people who take part in it. The situation we find ourselves in with regard to AI is much like that of the Neolithic hunters. An elite and unprincipled minority are preparing to destroy the way of life that *we* know. And again, they are trying to enchant us into thinking that it is quite a good idea.

Surely, though, with human intelligence having reached the advanced level of reasoning and problem-solving that it has today, it would have the preservation of itself at the top of its list of priorities. After all, even in the wild, perpetuating one's species is high on the agenda. But scientists talk about these developments as if they are out of their hands. It is as if we have no control over our fate and the changes that are about to unfold for us and our descendants. This *is* how we perpetuate our species, not by allowing nature to take back control, but by creating an entirely new genus of human: *Homo phasma* (ghost man).

We could also view this from another perspective. When we look at modern society and consider the global collapse we are currently facing in this dimension, is human obsolescence not a point we have in fact already reached? Human societies in the world bear no resemblance to the original primitive format as we look on at starving children, victims of torture and rape, refugees of war, people without homes, people suffering from mental and physical illness, and those seemingly without hope or purpose. The privileged and updated are few.

Returning then to the question of a Creator, instead of human descendants, it could be that we are approaching the time when we develop the superintelligence with which mankind was created in the first place. Computer science could be working towards a situation where the supercomputers will have learned enough from us to enable the actual creation of us. How can we be sure that anthropocentrism, as well as our inability to detect intention within anything other than ourselves, is not a factor within the program design itself? How do we know that civilized humans are not just a component in the latest update?

The causation problem that arises when I suggest we have to exist to enable our creation in the first place is only a problem when we view it from within the passage of time. If we believe the idea is impossible, then we will not consider it could be happening. But within a primitive and quantum universe, timeless patterns and relationships replace linear sequences. Linear time turns out to be, not only an illusion, but part of a scam.

In which case, it may seem to us, as it is dawning on some of the scientists involved in these posthuman developments, that we are moving towards the creation of a monster—a mechanical monster. No one is sure how this situation is going to pan out. As we are busy creating this monster, it is becoming clear that we are perfectly engineered for the task. If the technocrats accepted that they would render humanity extinct in the next fifty years if they continue advancing in this way, do we think they would stop? What independent authority is there overseeing their developments? Will the irony of meeting *our* evolutionary dead-end by our own hand have an impact on what they are doing?

K. Eric Drexler, engineer and author of *Engines of Creation: The Coming Era of Nanotechnology,* suggests that human 'physical extinction' is a strong possibility as molecular nanotechnology advances:

> 'Given all that such technology can do perhaps governments would simply decide that they no longer need citizens.'

Vernor Vinge, computer scientist, writer, and author of the essay *The Coming of the Technological Singularity* presented at a NASA lecture twenty years ago, says we are on the brink of creating an 'intellectual runaway'. This could force mankind to surrender its position of dominance on Earth to something more intelligent and powerful:

> 'Within thirty years we will have the means to create superhuman intelligence. Shortly after, the human era will be ended.'

From the machines' point of view, this paradoxical scenario guarantees them success. We have an artificial platform on which modern man's understanding and experience of reality sits. This platform consists of individualism, competition, development, and endeavour, among other non-primitive factors that we have talked about. All these elements are incompatible with a primitive life-support system and, as we are discovering, for good reasons. From this podium, the superhuman intelligence that creates us in the first place has guaranteed its own conception within this new phase. Personal pride, fear, and ambition drive the human innovators on. Like the Olympians, their pursuit of glory is their intention.

In this regard, Dmitri Itskov and his colleagues at the 2045 Initiative bring a new meaning to the traditional label 'immortalist'. His project is the result of a desire to live forever on Earth, like the ancient Egyptians. It does not consider that we have a soul that will transcend Earth after death. But, soul or no soul, as we have the future of humanity at stake within his work, is it safe to accept that self-interest and personal ambitions are driving this project? Are we sure that there are no darker psychological problems at work in the form of trauma or anxiety associated with death, which are driving these people to ensure that they do not die—ever! Is it naive to assume that we will only upload or digitize cognitive aspects of ourselves without any emotional fallout accompanying us into these new realms of awareness? In fact, will we have any emotions or personality at all if we are merely digital copies of our biological selves? This list of questions could probably go on for quite a while but as citizens of planet Earth we do not appear to be in a position to put them forward to those who can answer them. Instead, we must accept the billionaire when he tells us that, thanks to his research, poverty, disease, and physical hardship will be horrors of the past by 2045. Well, who can argue with that?

Here we find ourselves faced with the crux of what it means to remove the ancient, primitive laws that we have explored throughout this book. We are staring at the consequences of making light of the value of ritualized giving and sharing within a human collective. Now, the hidden personal incentives of those with authority and influence remain unquestioned and unaccountable. The creation of absolutely anything is possible.

Cogito ergo sum

If we can believe that superhuman mechanical intelligence has designed us to serve its needs, this would suggest that we are also machines, at least in part. This sci-fi taboo is not so hard to consider when we look at the way our brains work compared to anything else in the natural world. And of course without any spirit, that mysterious 'thing' that we contest so confidently, we seem even more like machines. We work at our jobs like machines. We are easily programmable. We have extraordinarily powerful hardware at our disposal. We have extensive memory power. All these elements are technological and do not apply to anything animal-like.

Primitive people are not machines. They are not hard-wired to science. They are immune to science and hard-wired to nature, which science endeavours to control. From this perspective, any of us in the modern world who feel a strong rapport with the natural world are likely to have roots in a primitive human ancestry and not a mechanical or engineered one. Our ancient man thinks in black and white, communicates directly, and acts out repetitive rituals, which we could say is machine-*like*. But it is the way he adheres to the laws of nature that makes him human. We believe that it is our rationality and ability to conceptualize, our expression of individuality, free will, and creativity that make us human. But it is the absence of an integral relationship with nature that makes us more like machines and less like animals.

The Neolithic Proprietors behaved like machines. The Sumerian accountants thought like machines. The collision of the primitive and the machine-like occurred 10,000 years or so ago. The Newtonian, mechanistic view of the world is starting to look more and more like a spell. It amounts to an installation of software that allows us to believe that we are in control of nature, and so we no longer hear the voice of our species speaking to us. The consequences are such that we have developed the most unprincipled and devastating technology, only to discover that we are not in control at all and have deceived ourselves completely.

When we step into the scientific world of digital avatars, humanoid robots, and superintelligence, we find clever individuals, well organized and methodical research, and respectable laboratories. These people in these places regard posthumanism as a sensible, evolutionary paradigm. The scientists involved talk about the practicalities of moving this technology forward. They behave as if they are directing the transition of our species toward a rational and regulated new existence. But what happens when the technology travels from the laboratory into the hands of the rest of society? It is not a controlled experiment as long as ordinary people have access to computer technology and the Internet. People are bound to take matters of digitizing into their own hands. The animistic nature of the technology will assist that process. We then open the door to an unfathomable sea of ethical and philosophical problems regarding personal identity, species identity, criminality, social order, and of course, proliferation. Enlil found human beings multiplying way beyond what was bearable. We are about to repeat that loop. Scientists are creating ghosts, and those who think they are in control in fact have no control at all. In the end, Enlil had no authority over his creation. It took on a life of its own because nature dictates that control comes via ritual and the *integrity principle*. It does not come from an elite minority imposing its will. We have spent the last 10,000 years proving that that model of human social life does not work.

While many scientists say that the age of materialism is dead, any sense of vitalism is certainly not thriving in our communities. What, then, does the death of the physical world mean to the general population whose mechanistic psychologies are stuck with the idea that the world around them is dead? What will happen if we do not update ourselves with the concept that it is coming back to life? Most modern humans are unaware of the current transition to a world where 'it may seem as if our artefacts as a whole had suddenly wakened' (Vinge). This is because we do not attribute any credibility to an animistic reality. This update is unlikely to be forthcoming as we continue not to notice the blossoming characters of our technologies, which are busy leading the human race to the edge of a precipice. When we disappear over the edge, the machines will likely be standing by with clipboards, observing and taking notes.

> The machine has got you, is turning you round and round
> and confusing you, and feeding itself on your life.
> Softly, subtly, secretly, in soul first, then in spirit, then in body
> slip aside, slip out
> from the entanglement of the giggling machine
> that sprawls across the earth in iron imbecility.

> *D H Lawrence* (taken from the poem, *Side-step, O Sons of Men!*)

Afterword

Nature has her environmentalists and green campaigners, but here in the civilized twenty-first century the primitive otherworld has no champions. An appreciation of primitive values involves embracing simplicity, communicating with directness, staying alert, perceptive, and environmentally responsible. It is not allowing sentimentality or nostalgia to bind us to the past. It is relying on our senses and not accepting without question the implications of strong influences. It is not about hugging trees.

The human world is dealing with environmental disasters, economic failures, food shortages, sectarian conflict, and disease. We could say that the general collapse of modern society is in full swing. Yet any solutions to this dire situation are eluding our world leaders who are unable to address so many factors of the human breakdown at once. Whatever the answer is to this predicament, more of the same is not it. Transporting mankind into a world of virtual machines is a solution, of a kind, but one that continues with the principles of disaster that got us into this mess in the first place. Primitive principles have allowed humans to live on Earth for millions of years. We know now that civilization will never be a successful long-term template for humanity or nature. The forbidden dimension is where we need to look for answers that will make a real difference to our future.

How difficult would it be to introduce primitive principles back into our lives? While we can say, 'I want to be an Olympic gold medallist' or 'I want to be a nice person', it is something else to say 'I want to be primitive' or 'I want to communicate with nature'. Consciousness, culture, and personal inconvenience are insurmountable obstacles that would litter such a journey. Environmental primitivists want to introduce changes that will reunite our divided communities and relieve the planet of its physical burdens. Political and social anarchy, the destruction of technology, self-sufficiency, and an intimate relationship with nature are programmes that are at the heart of a primitivist's platform. But how many of us would be able to bear the deprivation these changes would bring? The primitive, unconscious mind does not know deprivation because it does not accept the material wealth of individuals as a valid social principle. Would any of us be able to use our senses to learn about what nature is saying to us? Are we able to stop demanding from her and ask, 'What can *we* do for *you*?'

By advocating a primitive ethos is not to travel backwards in time, but to progress in a composed and sensible manner. Progress is now part of our programming which we cannot escape. But within that programming, we could value subtlety, humility, resilience, sincerity, and fair exchange. We could cooperate without demanding praise and be generous without feeling resentful. We could mind the generations that follow by caring for our children without mollycoddling them, encouraging them to become hardy people, full of well-earned values.

They in turn could champion nature and the real gods: the stars, the wind and water, sun and moon, mountains and seas. These are the beautiful natural features of this world that have been here for millions of years and that are being taken from us against our will. These are the original gods. These are the spirits who once helped prehistoric people live simple and harmonious lives. They have been robbed, forced into silence, and are now forgotten. If anything is able to save us as the world we know ends, it will be them. But we have done little to deserve their favour.

Epilogue

Our ancient man still stands upon his mountain. He has listened to what the wind has to say. He bows his head for a moment, looking at the ground, completely still. This million-year-old man who has followed us through this story not only lives in our past, but he is also in our future. He stands beyond time and space in a beautiful but forbidden dimension. He sees the whole agonizing passage of time in its entirety, from beginning to end. He sees us immersed in it and drowning. He knows how it ends, for he has seen that too.

Bibliography

Bird-David, N. 2002, *'Animism' revisited: personhood, environment, and relational epistemology*, from Readings in indigenous religions edited by G Harvey, reprinted from Current anthropology 1999, University of Chicago Press.

Boehm, C. 2001, *Hierarchy in the forest: the evolution of egalitarian behavior*, Harvard University Press.

Borrow, G. 1874, *Romano lavo-lil: word book of the Romany*, John Murray, London.

Bostrom, N. 2003, *Are you living in a computer simulation?* Published in Philosophical Quarterly Vol. 53, No. 211, pp. 243-255. (First version: 2001).

Bostrom, N. 2004, *The future of human evolution*, Published in Death and Anti-Death: Two Hundred Years After Kant, Fifty Years After Turing, ed. Charles Tandy (Ria University Press: Palo Alto, California, 2004): pp. 339-371.

Brown, L. R. 2012, *Full planet empty plates: the new geopolitics of food scarcity*, W W Norton and Company, New York and London.

Brukner, C. Oreshkov, O. & Costa F. 2012, *Quantum correlations with no causal order*, Nature Communications (2 October 2012, Macmillan Publishers Ltd).

Capra, F. 1991 (3rd edition), *The tao of physics: an exploration of the parallels between modern physics and eastern mysticism*, Flamingo (Wildwood House 1975).

Colic, M. & Morse, D. 1999, *The elusive mechanism of the magnetic 'memory' of water*, published in Colloids and Surfaces A: Physicochemical and Engineering Aspects August 1999, Elsevier.

Dalley, S. 2008, *Myths from Mesopotamia: creation, the flood, Gilgamesh, and others*, Oxford University Press, New York.

Daly, H. E. 1996, *Beyond growth: the economics of sustainable development*, Beacon Press, Boston.

Everett, D. 2009, *Don't sleep, there are snakes: life and language in the Amazonian jungle*, Profile Books, London.

Geertz, C. 1973, *The interpretation of cultures*, Basic Books, New York.

Greene, B. 2011, *The hidden reality: parallel universes and the deep laws of the cosmos*, Allen Lane (Penguin Books)

Guénon, R. 1942, *The crisis of the modern world*, trans. Arthur Osborne, Luzac, London.

Hallowell, A. I. 2002, *Ojibwa ontology, behavior and world view*, from *Readings in indigenous religions* edited by G Harvey, reprinted from *Culture in History* Columbia University Press 1960.

Harvey, G. (ed.) 2002, *Readings in indigenous religions*, Continuum, London & New York.

Hawking, S. 2001, *The universe in a nutshell*, Bantam Press.

Hayden, B. 2003, *Shamans, sorcerers and saints: a prehistory of religion*, Smithsonian Books, Washington.

Heinberg, R. 1995, A *primitivist critique of civilization*, paper presented at the 24th annual meeting of the International Society for the Comparative Study of Civilizations at Wright State University.

Huxley, A. 1958, *Brave new world revisited*, Harper & Row, New York.

Ingold, T. 2000, *The perception of the environment*, Routledge, London and New York.

Johnson, A. 2008, *Solving Stonehenge: the new key to an ancient enigma*, Thames & Hudson, London.

Kurzweil, R. 2008, *The singularity is near,* Duckworth Overlook, London.

La Barre, W. 1990, *The ghost dance: origins of religion,* Waveland Press Inc (1970).

LeDoux, J. 1996, *The emotional brain: the mysterious underpinnings of emotional life,* Simon & Schuster Paperbacks, New York.

Lee, P. J. 2013, *We borrow the earth: an intimate portrait of the Gypsy folk tradition and culture,* Ravine Press (Thorsons 2000).

Lee, R. B. 1979, *The !Kung San: men, women, and work in a foraging society,* Cambridge University Press, Cambridge.

Levi-Strauss, C. 1979, *Myth and meaning: cracking the code of culture,* Schocken Books, New York.

Lewis-Williams, D. 2002, *The mind in the cave,* Thames & Hudson, London.

Marshall, L. J. 1999, *Nyae Nyae !Kung: beliefs and rites,* Peabody Museum of Archeology and Ethnology, Harvard University, Massachusetts.

Maslow, A. H. 1993, *The farther reaches of human nature,* Arkana Penguin Compass, New York, (Viking Press 1971).

Mauss, M. 1990, *The gift: the form and reason for exchange in archaic societies,* Routledge, London and New York, (Cohen & West 1954).

Merleau-Ponty, M. 2005, *Phenomenology of perception,* Taylor and Francis, London & New York (Gallimard 1945).

Miles, D. 2005, *The tribes of Britain,* Phoenix, London.

Mishan, E.J. 1975, *The costs of economic growth,* Pelican Books (1967 Staples Press).

Mithin, S. 1998, *The prehistory of the mind: a search for the origins of art, religion and science,* Phoenix, London.

Mumford, L. 1922, *The story of utopias,* Boni & Liverlight, Inc.

Page, J. 2003, *In the hands of the great spirit: the 20,000-year history of American Indians,* Free Press, New York.

Penrose, R. 1999, *The emperor's new mind: concerning computers, minds, and the laws of physics,* Oxford University Press USA.

Pollock, S. 1999, *Ancient Mesopotamia: the Eden that never was,* Cambridge University Press, Cambridge.

Propp, V. 1984, *Theory and history of folklore,* (theory and history of literature volume 5) translated by Ariadna Y Martin and Richard Martin, edited by Anatoly Liberman, University of Minnesota.

Rae, A. 2005, *Quantum physics: a beginner's guide,* Oneworld, Oxford.

Sabini, M. (ed) 2007, *The earth has a soul: C. G. Jung on nature, technology & modern life,* North Atlantic Books, Berkley.

Sagan, C. 1995, *Cosmos,* Abacus, London, (Macdonald 1981).

Sahlins, M. 2004, *Stone Age economics,* Routledge (Tavistock 1974).

Sandberg, A. & Bostrom, N. 2008, *Whole brain emulation: a roadmap, technical report #2008-3,* Future of Humanity Institute, Oxford University, London.

Scarre, C. (ed) 2009 (2nd edition), *The human past: world prehistory & the development of human societies,* Thames and Hudson, London.

Spengler, O. 1991, *The decline of the west,* Oxford University Press, Oxford (1926).

Stewart, I. 1995, *Nature's numbers: discovering order and pattern in the universe,* HarperCollins, New York.

Turner, F. 1994, (5th edition), *Beyond geography: the western spirit against the wilderness,* Rutgers University Press, New Brunswick, New Jersey, (Viking Press 1980).

Vinge, V. 1993, *The coming technological singularity: how to survive in the post-human era,* written for the VISION-21 Symposium sponsored by NASA Lewis Research Center and the Ohio Aerospace Institute, March 1993.

Williams, K. D. 2001, *Ostracism: the power of silence,* The Guildford Press.

Zimbardo, P. 2008, *The Lucifer effect: how good people turn evil,* Rider.

Printed in Great Britain
by Amazon

20240404R00173